IN THE COURT OF THE
JADE EMPEROR

In the Court of the Jade Emperor

Stories from Old China

NEW EDITION

Rosalind Kerven

CAMBRIDGE
UNIVERSITY PRESS

Cambridge Reading

General Editors
Richard Brown and Kate Ruttle

Consultant Editor
Jean Glasberg

PUBLISHED BY THE PRESS SYNDICATE OF THE UNIVERSITY OF CAMBRIDGE
The Pitt Building, Trumpington Street, Cambridge CB2 1RP, United Kingdom

CAMBRIDGE UNIVERSITY PRESS
The Edinburgh Building, Cambridge CB2 2RU, United Kingdom
40 West 20th Street, New York, NY 10011-4211, USA
10 Stamford Road, Oakleigh, Melbourne 3166, Australia

First published 1993
This edition published 1999

Printed in the United Kingdom at the University Press, Cambridge

Typeset in Concorde

A catalogue record for this book is available from the British Library

ISBN 0 521 63524 1 paperback

Cover illustration by Sam Thompson
Text illustrations by Bryna Waldman

Contents

The Extraordinary Adventures of Monkey   7
Part One   In which Monkey proves that nothing is impossible   9
Part Two   In which Monkey gets too big for his boots   15
Part Three   In which Monkey tastes the Peaches of Immortality   21
Part Four   In which Monkey takes a giant leap to nowhere   25

The Sun, the Moon and the Stars   31
Woman-of-the-Moon, Man-of-the Sun   33
The Farmer and the Goddess   37
Darkness   41
The Palace of Boundless Cold   45

The Realms of the Dragons   49
The Golden Key   51
The Man Who Did Dragons' Work   57
The Hot Pig and the Dragon Princess   61

Roads to Heaven   67
The Girl Who Went Her Own Way   69
Cakes and Kitchens   73
Storm Girl   77
The Boys Who Lost Their Time   81

About the People Who Told these Stories   85

Sources   92

The Extraordinary
Adventures of Monkey

PART ONE

In which Monkey proves that nothing is impossible

First there was just a rock. The sun warmed it. Then there was magic. The rock cracked open like an egg. And Monkey jumped out!

How can a living creature hatch out of stone? Who understands the ten thousand things, the mysteries? Yet this is how it happened.

Monkey thought to himself, I'm impossible! No-one has ever been born this way before. It must mean that, for me, *nothing* is impossible! Fantastic! I'm going to be the greatest creature that ever lived! One day, I shall rule the whole Earth. More than that, why shouldn't I take over Heaven too?

This thought made him bubble with excitement, until he broke into a crazy, leaping dance.

Just then a crowd of other, ordinary monkeys came by. They all stopped and stared at him. Not one had ever before seen anyone look so happy. There was something quite irresistible about him that made them all queue up to shake his paw and slap him on the back and ask him to be their friend.

Monkey was delighted. Very soon, and without even trying, he had gathered together hundreds – no thousands – of friends and followers.

"How about making me your king?" laughed Monkey. "I promise I can protect you from every conceivable danger. If you just agree to listen to what I tell you, and always obey me, I swear that in return I will always give you everything you need."

At this, all the ordinary monkeys let out a great cheer. In no time, some of them had made a throne for Monkey to sit on. Then they all made a great ceremony of bowing down before him, and clapping and shouting "Long live King Monkey!"

The centre of the new kingdom was a marvellous stone palace, surrounded by gardens. It had unlimited space: everyone who wanted to could live there. It was hidden from the outside world by the wet, shining curtain of a waterfall.

The new king was absolutely thrilled. Oh yes, how he loved to be totally in charge and boss everyone else about. Every single one of his subjects was happy too, for there was always plenty to eat; and a party of some kind seemed to be held in the palace almost every day. What a life!

And yet, and yet . . . All things in Earth and Heaven must change.

One night, King Monkey was presiding over a wonderful banquet, surrounded by sumptuous flowers and fruit, when suddenly he burst into noisy tears.

"Your majesty!" shouted all his subjects in dismay, "tell us whatever is wrong? How can we possibly comfort you?"

King Monkey held up a solemn paw.

"My friends," said he, "listen, for I have really terrible news. I am growing old! One day I shall actually die! Then I will not see any of you, ever again – and you will not see me. Oh, isn't it awful? And the worst thing is that no-one can possibly save me from this fate."

At this, many of the other monkeys also began to weep in sympathy. But there was one small, humble fellow who ran urgently up to the king and begged him to listen.

"Your majesty," he whispered, "do not despair, for your fate isn't quite sealed yet. Haven't you heard that there are supposed to be people around who have discovered the secret of everlasting life?"

A silence fell upon the hall. Into it, King Monkey said, "Yes. I have heard . . . rumours of this. But can they possibly be true? Who are these amazing people?"

"They are most certainly true, my lord!" said the little fellow excitedly. "Few, yet many are those who know this secret. They are called the *Immortals*."

"Indeed!" exclaimed King Monkey. He sat up very straight and his eyes began to sparkle again. "So! Tell me, little friend, where may I find these exceptional people?"

"They live far away, here and there, your majesty, in ancient caves amongst enchanted hills. Look hard enough, and surely you will find them in the end."

Scarcely had King Monkey heard these encouraging words than he had leaped up from the table, and was off to prepare himself for a very long journey. The next day saw him exchanging fond goodbyes with his dear subjects. Then he climbed onto a raft and sailed away.

After many days, he came at last to the distant borders of the Southern Continent. There he disguised himself as a man and wandered amongst human beings, hoping that someone could point him in the right direction. But (oh, disappointment!) the people who lived in this land were all so engrossed in trying to become rich or famous that they had no time to spare for thinking about the great mysteries of life and death.

The years turned. Monkey wandered and travelled on, and ever onwards, never losing sight of his quest. Next he reached the shores of the Western Ocean. He sailed across it and came to the Western Continent.

There were hills and mountains here, that rose to the sky, covered with dark forests and blue drifting mists. Monkey walked on and up, climbing high into the towering peaks until he came upon a woodcutter dressed in torn old rags.

This man was singing away as he worked, as if he had not a care in the whole world.

"Good morning, Mr Woodcutter," called Monkey. "That's a happy song."

"It is indeed," replied the cutter, "for the man who taught it to me is more than happy."

"Oh," said Monkey, "and why is that?"

The cutter winked at him. "Well friend. He has the *knowledge*. You know. *The great secret.*"

"You mean . . .?" exclaimed Monkey.

"I do indeed, my friend." The cutter glanced around and lowered his voice. "He's an Immortal. He's found . . . everlasting life."

Monkey squealed with excitement. "At long, long last! The very man, the very thing that I've been searching everywhere for, these last nine years! Tell me, Mr Woodcutter, would he ever share this secret with anyone?"

The cutter grinned. "Well! He always has a load of students hanging around him, hanging on his every word, doing all his dirty work for him: the housework and washing and so on. He's put out the idea that, if they stick around in his presence for long enough, they might get to discover the great secret too. Not that I've ever heard of anyone who actually did. He keeps them all too busy skivvying, fetching his firewood and water and the like, to have much chance to advance in spiritual matters."

"Nevertheless," said Monkey, "I am confident that he will share his secret with *me*. For listen to this, Mr Woodcutter: *I* am the greatest being that ever lived!"

"Oh, and are you now?" said the woodcutter, spluttering sceptically as he turned back to his work. "Well Monkey, if you think you can really wangle the magic formula or whatever it is out of him, Father Subodhi is the man you're looking for. You'll find his house way across there, on Holy Terrace Mountain at the Cave of the Slanting Moon."

Monkey thanked him, and went on. Soon he came to the very cave. There a fairy-boy welcomed him and took him in to the old Immortal himself, who after much grumbling agreed to accept him as a pupil.

For the next seven years, Monkey stayed there. All that time, he was compelled to study hard and work even harder. To be quite frank, it did him a power of good. He was so busy with trying to understand obscure verses of the holy scriptures, and helping with the heavy household and garden chores, that he had almost no time to spare for merry-making or mischief.

But of course nothing could keep Monkey down for ever. One day, when Father Subodhi was lecturing his students on some solemn subject of deepest mystery, he was shocked to see Monkey dancing up and down before him, and singing at the top of his voice!

"What is the meaning of this disgusting and insulting behaviour?" the old Immortal roared.

Monkey stopped dancing. He looked Father Subodhi in the eye and grinned. "It has a *secret* meaning, master," he said. "Do you wish to know it?"

The Immortal narrowed his eyes and returned his gaze.

"You know the answer to that as well as I do," he said softly. "Now – get out!"

Monkey went. But in the darkest watches of the night he returned, creeping along to Father Subodhi's private room. The Immortal was expecting him. Smiling behind his wispy beard, he invited Monkey to sit down.

"I won't waste your precious time, sir," said Monkey at once, "so let me tell you my secret. I have the gift of a remarkable destiny: I am going to become master of Earth and of Heaven!"

The Immortal nodded but made no reply, and his ancient face remained inscrutable. Monkey licked his lips and went on.

"Great teacher, in order to achieve this destiny, I must have access to the secret knowledge that you guard so carefully in your heart. The time is ripe: I have come to ask you to share it with me."

"So, Monkey," answered the Immortal, "you really wish to know the secret of everlasting life?"

"I have wandered and waited, year after long year, to learn it," answered Monkey. "I refuse to give up. I must achieve my aim."

"Very well then, Monkey. Listen carefully to what I tell you. After you have listened, learn it. And after you have learned it, understand it. This short verse contains everything:

All magic grows within you: deep.
Spirit, breath and soul are all your own.
Coil them like a spring, then keep
them tightly. They will yield the strongest powers known."

Monkey listened carefully. He repeated the verse over and over, until it was imprinted firmly into his head and his heart. Then he thanked Father Subodhi and went away.

For a long time after that, he sat alone very quietly, thinking, meditating on this short lesson. At length, the curious words lost their humdrum shape and became as sharp as dream images, charged with a magic power that suddenly surged hotly through his limbs. At that moment, his whole body felt as if it were floating in golden light and youthful strength.

Monkey rushed back to find Father Subodhi. The Immortal saw at once that Monkey had found his magic powers. He smiled and nodded.

"Now then, young fellow! All that remains is to teach you the magic

13

formula to perform seventy-two different transformations. Practise this carefully, and within no time at all you will be able to turn yourself into anything you want, from a tree to a demon's double. Oh yes, and I must also teach you how to fly on a cloud trapeze, so fast that a single leap will carry you head over heels, 108,000 leagues. Finally, you had better learn how to ward off the Three Calamities. Which are: being struck by lightning, devoured by fire, or melted by wind. Certainly when you know all this, Monkey, you will be well on the way to achieving your ambition of being invincible, and to mastering Heaven as well as Earth."

So Monkey practised yet more secret words over and over, until he knew them all by heart. You can imagine how much he relished turning himself into seventy-two different shapes! And he could scarcely wait to try travelling right round the world in a few simple bounds.

When he was sure he had mastered it all, he thanked Father Subodhi again and gave him a great hug.

"Now I know for sure that nothing in the world is difficult," he exclaimed. "It is only our own thoughts that make things seem so."

Father Subodhi smiled thinly.

"Well, cheerio, great teacher!" And with those words, Monkey hopped onto his new cloud trapeze and leaped away . . .

"Wait!" called Father Subodhi. "Let me give you a word of advice. Take care Monkey . . . Beware! You must use your new powers carefully. If you don't . . ."

But even if Monkey heard, he pretended not to.

And if you want to know what became of him next, read on!

PART TWO

In which Monkey gets too big for his boots

Monkey flew straight home on his cloud. He couldn't wait to show off his new tricks to all his subjects. But as soon as he arrived, he had a terrible shock. An evil demon had stormed his palace! He had stolen absolutely everything he could lay his hands on and – worst of all – kidnapped most of the monkey children.

Perhaps you think Monkey was dismayed? Not a bit. Instead, he rubbed his paws together and said to himself,

"Ahah, here's a grand chance to try out my new powers!"

So he jumped back onto his cloud trapeze and directed it straight to the jagged mountain top where the demon lived. There he was spotted at once by a crowd of the villain's imps, who yelled for their foul master to hurry to the scene.

"Oh-hoh, oh-hee-hee," sneered the demon. "What have we here, eh? Another measly little wimp of a monkey. Come into my lair, you pathetic worm, and let me fatten you up with the others for my feast."

"Don't be so hasty," snapped Monkey. "Don't you realise you've just insulted the greatest creature on Earth?" And he held up his fists for a fight.

At this, the demon shook with deafening convulsions of laughter. Nevertheless, he accepted the challenge. After a few minutes of fighting bare-fisted, he was astonished to realise that Monkey, slight as he looked, was actually winning.

In a panic, the demon snatched up his sword and came at Monkey with it.

Poor Monkey: he had flown there so quickly that he had no weapon whatsoever to hand. But no matter, here was his chance to transform!

He took a deep breath; he held it deep within himself. Then he

15

plucked out a handful of his own hairs. He put them in his mouth; he spat them out again; he shouted, "Change!"

At once, the hairs turned into hundreds of miniature Monkeys, each one as fierce and energetic as himself!

The miniature ones were everywhere, darting about, stinging like mosquitoes. Within no time at all, they had slain the demon and every one of his imp soldiers.

As soon as their task was completed, Monkey said the returning spell and the miniature ones turned back into hairs.

Then he tried out some more magic. It all worked splendidly. His first spell found and freed the imprisoned monkey children. His second spell carried them home with him. His third spell restored his old palace back to its great, luxurious glory.

Of course, all his subjects were absolutely thrilled to welcome him back after so many years. They were especially relieved to know that they still had a strong king to take care of them. And yet . . .

"We must never let such a disaster happen again," Monkey told them firmly. "I'm afraid that the days when we used to do nothing but play and party all day long are finished. My kingdom and my people must grow up now, and learn to live in the real world. You are all going to have to learn to fight for yourselves."

He selected 47,000 of the bravest and strongest monkeys to form a proper army and equipped them with the latest types of weapons.

Soon, news of their might spread right round the continent. Now all the neighbouring kings, all the wild beasts, and even the demons came to pay homage to Monkey's kingdom. They all spoke of his army with the greatest respect and fear.

Not surprisingly, this fame and success soon went to Monkey's head. He took to strutting around and boasting, "I am the greatest king the Earth has ever known!" and "I'm well and truly master of the world!" and so on, all day long, until even his best friends and closest advisers got fed up with hearing it.

"He needs something new to distract him," they said. And before long, Monkey himself hit upon the very thing. It was a new weapon.

"None of the usual sort of weapons is really good enough for someone as powerful and immortal as me," he complained. "I need something as exceptional as myself, something imbued with magic powers equal to my own."

His ministers and advisers discussed the problem privately until they thought of a good solution. Then the Chief Minister went to Monkey saying, "Your majesty, we recommend that you approach the Dragon King of the Eastern Sea. We have heard that he has the most magnificent collection of weapons to be found on Earth – or, indeed, in Heaven. We are sure he would consider . . ."

Without waiting to hear any more, Monkey cast a quick spell to protect himself from the water; then ran down to the sea and jumped in.

On the sea bottom, he was welcomed by a grand procession, with the Dragon King at its head, followed by all his dragon children and grandchildren. Next came a line of shrimp soldiers and crab generals; then finally a mass of servants, who were variously fish, turtles and eels.

They treated Monkey to an elaborate tea ceremony, after which the talk turned to the weapon he was wanting.

The Dragon King took him into his armoury and showed him any number of swords, spears, axes and cudgels; but Monkey turned his nose up at them all.

"I am most disappointed," he complained. "I was told you would offer me something outstanding. What are you hiding from me?"

The Dragon King sighed and shook his head. Then he went off to confer with his royal family. After much hissing and whispering, the old Dragon Mother Queen came to him saying, "Monkey, my dear, we do indeed have one more weapon that you haven't yet seen. However, we felt sure you would refuse it, for it is much too heavy for someone as, er, slim and, er, compact as yourself."

She clapped her hands and called out a command. A few minutes later, a hundred shrimp soldiers burst through the door, staggering under the weight of a gigantic metal staff.

"This," said the Dragon King, "is the Golden Clasped Wishing Staff. Long ago, the gods used it to pound the star-dust of the Milky Way. If you really want it, I suppose I could let you have it."

Monkey's eyes lit up. He mumbled some magic words. At once the Wishing Staff shrank to just the right size for his paw. He picked it up. He tested it in one paw, he rested it in the other. He swung it around his head. He gave a whoop of delight.

The Dragon royal family waited for him to thank them, and to offer some payment; but Monkey did neither.

Instead he said, in a whining voice, "This Wishing Staff is all very well, but aren't you going to offer me something suitably grand to wear with it?"

"Well, I have nothing of that kind for you," replied the Dragon King curtly.

"What?" screamed Monkey. "Nothing to offer the greatest creature on Earth, heh? Are you quite sure?"

He bared his teeth and aimed the Wishing Staff threateningly at the Dragon King's head.

"You'd better try your brothers my dear," whispered the Dragon Mother Queen.

The Dragon King nodded wearily. He called his speediest fish servants and gave them urgent messages to carry to the Dragon Kings of the Southern, Northern and Western Seas. For the next hour there was much hurried coming and going through mysterious water tunnels and by-ways.

The outcome of it was that Monkey was presented with a pair of cloud-stepping shoes made of lotus blossom; a cap made of red gold decorated with feathers from the fabled phoenix bird; and a chain-mail jerkin made of the purest yellow gold.

At last Monkey was satisfied, though he didn't have the manners to show it.

"About time too!" he yelled back at them as he rose up through the water. "I know you didn't really want me to have anything, you dirty old sneaks!"

Naturally, all his subjects were very impressed by the Wishing Staff. Monkey made sure that they spent ages watching the somewhat terrifying tricks he could do with it.

Meanwhile, the Dragon King of the Eastern Sea was left behind in a thundrous rage. He stormed straight up to Heaven, where he demanded an emergency audience with the Jade Emperor himself. He presented the ruler of Heaven with a long document listing all his complaints about Monkey's loutish manners and menacing behaviour. The Jade

Emperor studied the document long and carefully. He promised to bring Monkey to justice.

That night, as Monkey slept, he dreamed that he was seized and taken away, like a prisoner, to be judged by Yama, the grim King of Death.

Yama showed Monkey that his name was inscribed on the register of all those who were due to die that very night!

"What utter rubbish!" exclaimed Monkey. With one great heave, he broke free of his bonds and the guards that were holding him down. "You can't possibly kill me off, you old idiot. Have you forgotten, Yama, that I'm an Immortal now?"

Then he seized a brush and, with a single thick stroke, crossed his name right off the Register of Death.

At this point Monkey woke up in a cold sweat. His head was still echoing with King Yama's terrible curses. He jumped out of bed and immediately ordered an enormous banquet for breakfast to celebrate the fact that he was still alive.

For he knew very well that a dream like that is really a true vision of the spirit-world, showing exactly things that have really happened in that strange, shadowy other-realm.

Even while Monkey celebrated, the King of Death was making his own journey to Heaven. He too handed in a long, formal complaint about Monkey.

When the Jade Emperor had finished studying it, he realised that Monkey was a total menace and that he would have to take urgent action to control him.

No doubt you wonder what he did, and whether it worked. Well, turn to the next page!

PART THREE

In which Monkey tastes the Peaches of Immortality

Monkey was sitting on his throne feeling mighty pleased with himself as usual, when suddenly a strange old man swept in, unannounced.

"Good morning, Monkey," he said briskly and without so much as a bow. "I am the spirit of the Planet Venus. I represent the Jade Emperor, who commands you to come at once. I gather he has a job for you in the offices of Heaven."

Monkey jumped up. He was thrilled. Fancy being asked to go up to work with the gods in Heaven so soon! He hadn't realised how far his reputation had spread. He wasted no time in following Venus up into the sky. There, they hurried to the golden-doored Cloud Palace, and Monkey found himself standing before the Jade Emperor himself.

The ruler of Heaven stared at him in silence. Then he turned aside to mutter at some length with his advisers. At last he said, "Ah yes, Monkey. They have a vacancy in the royal stables for you."

The next moment, Monkey found himself being hustled away and fitted into the coarse uniform of a groom.

"Hang on," he protested, "don't you realise that I'm the greatest king on Earth? How dare you –?"

But instead of an answer, he felt someone shoving a spade into his hand and sending him along to muck out the horses' dung.

Of course, Monkey was having none of this. As soon as the supervisor's back was turned, he sneaked out, grabbed the nearest cloud trapeze and zoomed straight back to Earth.

"Dreadful place, Heaven," he said dismissively to anyone who asked him about it afterwards. And just to show what he thought of them 'up there', he issued a proclamation that, henceforth, he was to be known as the 'Great Sage, Equal of Heaven'.

Meanwhile, Heaven itself was in uproar. The Jade Emperor sent a whole troop of his spirit soldiers after Monkey, to arrest him. But when Monkey saw them brandishing weapons at him, he just burst out into raucous laughter and sent them packing with a handful of his easiest magic tricks.

So the spirit soldiers had to return to Heaven, very shame-faced, without him. The Jade Emperor was furious, shocked and perturbed. Who *was* this outrageous upstart?

He considered the problem for many days; he consulted his most valued counsellors and ministers; he studied the long and detailed reports they had compiled on Monkey's many misadventures. At last, the Jade Emperor came to the conclusion that it was impossible to contain the rogue by straightforward force. He would have to use more devious means.

A few days later, Venus appeared at Monkey's palace again. This time he handed over a very grand-looking scroll of paper. Monkey unfurled it and read:

Great Sage, Equal of Heaven:
The Jade Emperor hereby invites you to be Keeper of the Heavenly Peaches.
A new suite of luxury residential offices is exclusively available with this post.

"Ahah, this is a bit better!" squealed Monkey at once. "This is the sort of thing I've been waiting for."

And he sent his acceptance by return.

When he got back to Heaven, he was overjoyed to find that his new offices were even more splendid than he had expected. As for the work, it was almost non-existent: it seemed that no-one expected Monkey to do anything, except tick his name on an official list each day! Best of all, the offices were bang next door to the Heavenly Peach Garden.

Now, you must know that this was no ordinary garden. The 3,600 peach trees in it were all enchanted.

The fruit on the outer circle of trees ripened only once in a thousand years. Anyone who ate one of these peaches was at once transformed into a fairy. The middle trees grew peaches which ripened only once in six thousand years: those who ate them could fly through the air whenever they wanted, and besides would never grow old. But the trees in the centre were the rarest and most magical of all. They became ripe only once in nine thousand years; and anyone lucky enough to eat one of these would outlive all things on Heaven and Earth, and become imbued with the mystical powers which shine through the sun and the moon.

It's not hard to guess what Monkey did when he found himself in charge of all these! Each day, he took a slow, secret walk around the garden. And each day, he gobbled as many of the ripe fruits as he could find.

As a result – well, if he was simply immortal before – now, with his belly stuffed full of enchanted peaches, he became an absolute super-being!

Some time later, the Queen of Heaven decided to hold one of her famous Peach Banquets. Invitations were sent out to everybody who was anybody. Soon all the deities in Heaven were talking about it.

But Monkey wasn't invited.

First he felt miserable. Then he felt devastated. Then he flew into a blinding rage. What a snub! How dare they belittle him like this? Had they forgotten already that he was the Great Sage, Equal of Heaven?

Seething with anger, he jumped onto his cloud trapeze and set off, determined to ruin the Peach Banquet so that no-one else could enjoy it either.

When he arrived at the Queen's great hall, he found it full of servants, who were busily preparing the magic peach wine. The air was sweet with its exquisite, intoxicating scent. Monkey uttered a quick breathful of spells. Within seconds the servants fell, all together, into a deep, impenetrable sleep.

As soon as they were snoring, Monkey dived in and gulped down as much wine as he could. What he couldn't swallow, he spilled all over the floor. Oh, the wretch! Now, on top of everything else, he was utterly, despicably drunk.

His brain was heavy with a thick, stupid haze of flashing lights and dangerous incantations. Monkey decided he had better go back to his own place, to try to sleep it off. But he scarcely knew what he was doing, or where he was going. He took a wrong turning here, missed a road there . . .

. . . the end of it was that he found himself miles away from home, outside a large, mysterious mansion. A gold plate by the door named it as the house of Laozi – lord of *The Way and Its Power*: the master alchemist.

Monkey's head was clearing a little now. He shook himself. He noticed the door was slightly open. He peered inside. It was dark and still, dark and still.

Laozi must be out. Of course, *he* had been invited to the Peach Banquet. The thought gave Monkey a new pang of resentment. He glanced around, but the street was empty. He crept inside.

Curious, acrid smells wafted towards him. There were weird, bubbling noises. Monkey crept further in.

Through a second door, he found himself in a gloomy, circular room, where cauldrons and crucibles were steaming over low smoky fires that made him choke and cough. This must surely be Laozi's laboratory where he worked on the most mysterious secrets of alchemy. And the pots must surely be cooking his fabled Elixir of Immortality!

Monkey's heart was racing. Oh yes, now he could *really* work some mischief. Never mind those laborious techniques he'd learned from old Father Subodhi. Forget the rotten Peaches of Immortality. If he swallowed some of Laozi's extraordinary brew, he would probably end up immortal a million times over! This was better and better! He glanced round, grabbed the nearest ladle, and began to spoon the foul-tasting stuff into his mouth as fast as he could.

Aaaww! It was really strong, powerful stuff!

But at that moment a new thought suddenly made him stop in mid-gulp. He had remembered that Laozi was one of the most important gods in all of China – one of the most important gods *ever*. What would he do when he found that Monkey had burgled him? What would the Jade Emperor do?

Oh Monkey, no matter how immortal you are – now you're in for real trouble!

Monkey spluttered out the last of the Elixir. He muttered the hastiest spell he knew to make himself invisible. Then he turned his cloud trapeze straight towards Earth and sped down.

Do you think he got away with it this time? You'll have to find out in the next chapter.

PART FOUR

In which Monkey takes a giant leap to nowhere

Within a couple of days, every deity in Heaven was gossiping about Monkey's latest shocking behaviour. The Jade Emperor was in a frothing temper. He called up the entire Heavenly Army, and sent it down to Earth to surround Monkey's stone palace.

When Monkey saw the rows of spirit soldiers massed about his stronghold, armed to the teeth, he chuckled to himself. Then he went inside to fetch his Wishing Staff.

Swat! Swipe! Swish! It took only a handful of blows before the Heavenly Army was beaten to shreds and fleeing home in shame.

All the deities had been watching what happened. Now their despair plunged to new depths. Emergency meetings were held in every corner of Heaven; but no-one could think of a plan of action that would really work.

At last the Jade Emperor called up his nephew Erlang, the magician, whose outstanding skills had once enabled him to destroy six terrible ogres single-handed in one short battle.

Erlang was grinning as he flew down to tackle Monkey. And what a magnificent fight it turned out to be!

Erlang went into the attack shaped as a horrific, gigantic blue monster. As soon as he spotted him, Monkey turned into an exact copy of the same! Then Monkey darted away into the river, and transformed himself into a fish – at which Erlang turned into a cormorant and tried to gobble him up. Before he could do so, Monkey leaped up into the sky and then raced along to the magician's own house, where he transformed himself into Erlang's exact double!

The deities were watching the fight in great excitement, cheering Erlang on, and booing Monkey with every turn.

As soon as Monkey was inside the magician's house, Erlang shouted "Freeze!" At once, Monkey found he was turned to stone and could not move.

Then Laozi crept up, brandishing his enchanted Diamond Snare. He threw it down and – presto! – Monkey was caught.

The gods and goddesses were ecstatic. Laozi marched back in triumph, carrying Monkey, wriggling and squealing inside his net.

The Jade Emperor spoke in his most ominous voice.

"Take the wretch. Put him on the executioner's block. Cut him up into tiny pieces. Then throw the pieces away!"

So a troop of spirit soldiers threw him onto the block. But Monkey was indestructible, and when they tried to chop him up, they failed.

Then the Spirits of the Five Stars came along and tried to burn him with their cosmic fire. But Monkey was invincible, and they failed too.

Next, the Thunder Spirits approached, and pelted Monkey with a thousand million thunderbolts. But Monkey was unconquerable, and they failed as well.

Finally, Laozi picked Monkey up and put him into his Crucible of the Eight Trigrams. He slammed the lid down tightly and burned him in the white-hot flames of his alchemic fire for seven-times-seven days. But on the forty-ninth day, Monkey burst the lid off, jumped out and began to dart around Heaven like an irritating flea, swiping everyone he bumped into with his Wishing Staff.

The Jade Emperor paced up and down, fuming, seething, worrying about what to do next.

A messenger was despatched far, far away to the Western Paradise. He carried a desperate appeal to the Buddha (the Wise One, the Compassionate One), begging him to come and help.

And the Buddha came.

He sat calmly under a tree. He called Monkey to speak with him, and Monkey bounded up. He spoke in quiet, neutral tones, asking Monkey exactly what he was trying to achieve.

"Oh, that's quite simple, Buddha," boasted Monkey. "My aim is to cause such chaos that the Jade Emperor gets kicked off his throne. Then *I* can sit on it and become the ruler of Heaven."

"Ah," said the Buddha, shaking his round, smiling head, "but Monkey, do you really think you are clever enough to rule over Heaven? After all, the Jade Emperor has been perfecting himself and gathering wisdom for over two hundred million years."

Monkey guffawed. "What a slow-coach! Goodness me, I'm already much cleverer than him, and I've only been around for a fraction of the time."

"Is that so, Monkey?" said the Buddha. "Well then, let me challenge you to a wager. All I want you to do is this: jump across the palm of my right hand. If you succeed, the Jade Emperor's throne shall indeed be yours. But if you fail – oh, then Monkey, you must agree to a long and lonely punishment."

"Great," replied Monkey. "I accept, Buddha old chap. Ohoh, this is too easy! But just a minute – are you quite sure that you're really in a position to give me what you've promised?"

"Absolutely certain," smiled the Buddha.

He laid his hand upon the ground, palm up. It was about the size of a lotus leaf.

Monkey got ready. He shrunk his Wishing Staff to the size of a writing brush, and stuck it behind his ear. He crouched, he drew a deep breath, he shut his eyes, and he jumped.

Air sped past him. To those who watched, he moved so far that he seemed invisible. Remember, he could go 108,000 leagues in a single leap.

Within seconds, he had landed. Looking around, he saw a row of five pink pillars rising into the sky before him.

He said to himself, "Those must be the pillars that mark the very end of the world. I've jumped even further than I intended. Brilliant! – That stupid old Buddha can't help but be impressed."

He took the Wishing Staff from behind his ear and used it to inscribe upon the central pillar:

The Great Sage, Equal of Heaven,
reached this place.

Then, with a wicked chuckle, he made a large puddle of pee at the pillar's base as a mark of the profoundest disrespect.

Finally he turned an eye-dazzling somersault, which took him straight back, quick as a flash, to the spot from which he had started.

"OK Buddha my old mate," he said. "You saw me do it. Now, you'd better hurry up and hand me over the Jade Emperor's throne."

Slowly, still smiling, the Buddha shook his head.

"Monkey," he said, "that wasn't a bad try. What a shame that you failed."

"How dare you?" shrieked Monkey. "You sneak, you cheat! I jumped right across your hand, just like you said. You've got to keep your side of the bargain, Buddha."

"Do you mean you don't believe me?" said the Buddha. "But just look at my hand, Monkey."

He held it out. It was smeared with Monkey's dirty footprints. Something was scribbled in untidy characters on the middle finger. Monkey squinted at it and made out: *The Great Sage, Equal of Heaven, reached this place.* And gleaming in the crease where that finger joined the hand was a little pool of foul-smelling monkey pee.

"You see Monkey," said the Buddha sadly, "you only reached the base of my fingers. What you know is hardly anything; what you can do is nothing; and what you understand is the least of all."

Monkey stared at the hand. He stared at the Buddha. He looked down at himself and saw that, for all his vanity, in reality he was of less consequence than a speck of dust against the enormous, unfathomable mysteries of the Universe.

While Monkey was reflecting on this, the Buddha snapped his fingers. At once they were transformed into a mountain with five peaks. With his other hand he picked up Monkey and dropped him down a hole into the mountain's heart. Then he sealed the entrance tightly.

But the Buddha is always merciful. He appointed a guardian spirit to watch over Monkey, to protect him from harm, and to bring him food and drink.

And there King Monkey was forced to spend his punishment for 500 long years.

But don't shed any tears for him, reader. For I must tell you that, through those turning centuries, Monkey repented every bit of his wickedness and mischief.

As with all beings, the time came when he was reborn to a new life. He learned to tame and control his bad ways, and to use his extraordinary powers to do good.

Because of this, he was chosen by the gods to become a pilgrim. He went on a long and almost impossible journey, over unscalable mountains, through valleys beset with unspeakable dangers. He overcame eighty-one truly terrible perils.

On this journey, he accompanied a holy priest called Tripitaka, to the Rainbow Misted Mountain in the Western Paradise. There they fetched the holy scriptures of Buddhism and brought them back to China; and in this way they saved many people from evil and misery.

And at the very end, Monkey became a god.

Some of this story may be the truth. The remainder is like a mirror of truth. Hold it to the light, look in it and – who knows? – you may even find shreds of wisdom and the answers to certain mysteries reflected within.

The Sun, the Moon and the Stars

Woman-of-the-Moon, Man-of-the-Sun

In the whole of China, there was no-one who could destroy evil like Shenyi the archer.

Once, the forests had teemed with hideous, man-eating monsters; Shenyi's arrows had killed them all. Another time, nine blinding false suns had climbed into the sky to scorch and shrivel the land; Shenyi's arrows had melted them away.

He was fearless, superhuman. He could outwit any enemy, overcome any disaster.

Of course, he was the most famous man in China. The Emperor heaped him with honours.

But for Shenyi, no honour was enough.

He wanted to live in Heaven with the gods. He wanted to be immortal, to live for ever. He thought such rewards were his right.

But the gods refused to have him. They had mixed with him in the past, when he had caused deep trouble and arguments.

So Shenyi was left as he was, forever complaining about his situation to Chang'e, his wife. And day by day, Chang'e got tired of his continual boasting and bitterness.

"Shenyi," she said, "you always say you can do anything you want, no matter how difficult. If the gods in Heaven won't grant you immortality, what's stopping you from going out to find it for yourself?"

Now, you may have heard that there are many different paths that lead to this dream of everlasting life. Every way is shrouded in mystery. Most are secret, some are dangerous.

But to the truly brave, one way sounds simple enough. That is, to obtain some of the rare and fabled Elixir of Immortality; and then to swallow it.

Chang'e said, "Husband, I have heard that far, far away on Kunlun Mountain lives the monstrous Queen Mother of the West. It is rumoured that anyone who has enough power to cross her magic barriers of fire and water, and to scale the sheer sides of her mountain, has a good chance of persuading her to give them a taste of the brew she stirs in her cauldron. They say that this brew is, in fact, the longed-for Elixir of Immortality. Instead of grumbling, why don't you go to her and fetch some for yourself?"

Shenyi saw the sense of what she said. He set off at once. He travelled thousands of miles westward, until he came to the highest mountains on Earth. He strode up and across them as if they were ant-hills. No obstacle could stop him. At last he came to the dark cave of the goddess Queen Mother.

"Well then," she greeted him, "so it is the famous Shenyi! What do you want of me, archer?"

Shenyi looked steadily at her. Her face was that of an old woman, but her teeth were like a tiger's. Her body was covered in wild, matted hair, and ended in a leopard's tail. The jade crown upon her head was shaped like jagged sword blades.

"I have come to ask your majesty for a special favour. I would like some of your Elixir of Immortality."

"Do you really understand what you are asking for?" the old Queen Mother hissed back at him. "My Elixir is made from the fruit of an enchanted peach tree. These peaches only ripen one at a time, once every six thousand years. Each peach makes enough of my brew to satisfy only one person. If I were to give you what I have in my pot today, there would be none left for anyone else who seeks it for another six thousand years."

"There is no-one on Earth who needs this as much as I do," retorted Shenyi.

"Very well," said the Queen Mother, studying his face closely, "I shall let you have it. But I warn you to take great care with it, for it is strong and very dangerous stuff. Every peach that ripens contains different powers in its juice, and each one seems to be stranger than the last. I cannot tell you what is in this one; but I can warn you that what it does to you may not be at all what you expect; and once you have swallowed it, there is no going back."

Then she gave Shenyi a small box fastened tightly with a gold clasp and sent him home.

Chang'e was delighted to see him back with the Elixir. She asked to see it, but Shenyi only scorned her: "Silly woman, what could you understand of such powerful, spiritual things?"

Chang'e was offended. But she said nothing, for at that very moment, her heart began to beat fast and her senses quickened, as if Heaven itself were preparing her for something.

Shenyi hid the box in the roof of their house, choosing a place which she would never be able to reach. Then he took his bow and went out hunting.

Alone in the house, Chang'e sat quietly and waited.

Suddenly she saw a brilliant white light shining from a beam in the ceiling. The light turned into a tall ladder. She climbed up it. At the top, squeezed amongst the rafters of the roof, she saw the Queen Mother's box.

Chang'e wrenched the box from its hiding place and climbed down again. She prised open the lid. Inside lay a small, curiously coloured crystal.

Chang'e took it out and swallowed it.

At once, marvellous, frightening things began to happen. She felt her whole body grow light and transparent. She looked at her feet and found she was floating above the floor. Then very slowly, helplessly, like a piece of thistledown, she began to fly!

She flew out of the window. She rose up through the air. She rose above the sky. Away, away, away! At last, she came to land on a pale, empty, luminous world. It was the moon.

There was a white, shining palace waiting for her there, in a garden of sweet-smelling cinnamon trees. Chang'e went to live in it. She felt like a goddess-queen.

Finally she became transformed into the pure essence of *yin*: the mother of all things still, silent, quiet and mysterious.

Since then, her *yin* moon-power has always shone down to Earth. It waxes and wanes with her changing moods; it lights valleys and streams; it gives life to everything that is female.

When Shenyi came home and discovered his wife had swallowed the Elixir and flown off, his anger was as fearsome as his strength. He began to curse and storm about until his rage turned into a hurricane which swept him far, far away into the sky, to the place in the mountains where the God of the Immortals lived.

This god roared with laughter at Shenyi's curses.

"What's the point of being angry, archer? Everything that has happened was already decided in the Book of Fate. Stop stomping around, and eat this."

Servants came running in at his call and gave Shenyi a big red cake. Shenyi swallowed it whole. At once a roaring heat went surging through his body.

The god said, "This cake has given you the powers you need to equal and complement your wife. It is made to a special recipe to protect you from the fiercest heat of the sun. For the sun will be your new home, archer. Just as you longed for, everyone will be truly dazzled by your greatness up there!"

Then the god summoned an enormous bird, which he greeted as the Cock of Heaven. Shenyi climbed onto it, and it carried him to a golden palace on the sun.

There he became transformed into the pure essence of *yang*: the father of all things bright, active and strong.

Since then, his *yang* sun-power has shone in the sky. It lights the mountains and Heaven itself; it never wavers; it gives life to everything that is male.

The Farmer
and the Goddess

There was a young farmer who was terribly poor and terribly lonely. Although he toiled and sweated all day and half the night, he could get scarcely any crops at all to grow on his dried-up patch of land. In fact, the task would have been impossible without his ox. This animal was strong and good-natured. It pulled the plough for him; its dung helped to fertilise the wretched earth; and it was also his only companion.

One evening the farmer was wearily making the ox comfortable for the night before settling down himself, when he let out a long, sad sigh.

At once, a voice said, "Whatever is the matter, old friend?"

The young man jumped and gazed around in alarm. "Who's that?" he hissed into the shadows.

"It's me. Ox."

"You?" cried the farmer. "What...? Who...? Never! You can... *speak*?"

The ox took its own turn to sigh. "Ah, friend, I've got troubles too. Listen to this: once I was actually the Ox Star and I lived up in Heaven! Yes, I thought that would surprise you. But to cut a long story short, I got into bad trouble with the other gods because I was always acting slow and stupid, and I kept making really dreadful mistakes. So in the end they banished me, sent me down to live here on Earth, and made me work for a living. What a let down!"

The farmer was astonished and upset to hear his faithful companion's story. He patted him gently, while the ox went on:

"But I must say, you have always been very kind to me. Although you expect me to do all the heaviest work, you're always by my side and do more than your fair share. And you feed me well and always give me nice clean straw to sleep on. As punishments go, mine has been pretty easy going, thanks to you. So look friend, why don't you tell me what's upsetting you? I'd like to help you in return, if I possibly can."

The young man was lost for words for a few moments. Then he said, "Ox, I can cope with most of my misfortunes. The thing that really gets me down is the utter loneliness of my life. What I want more than anything is to get married. But there's no chance of any decent woman taking a fancy to a fellow as poor and ragged as me."

The ox gave a warm rumble of laughter. "Oh, the solution to that couldn't be easier! Have you heard of the Heavenly Maidens? No? Well, listen carefully. You know that on the edge of the forest there's that big, beautiful lake? Well, almost every night it's visited by these wonderful young ladies – real goddesses, straight from Heaven. They come down for a swim, you see, to get away for a while from all the petty rules and restrictions up there. Now then: if you go spy on them, and hide the clothes of the one you like best while she's splashing about, I can guarantee she'll fall madly in love with you. How about that, eh?"

The young farmer had never been so excited. The next evening he finished work early for the first time in ages. He had a good wash and brush up. Then he set off for the lake and hid in the bushes.

Very soon, he saw a dazzling shower of star-light. A crowd of young women came tumbling out of it, all laughing and chattering. They threw off their clothes and, in great merriment, plunged into the water. The farmer watched goggle-eyed.

They all looked so lovely! – much too good for him. But soon he found his eyes and his heart drawn to one who seemed quieter and gentler than the others.

His heart pounding, silently, slowly, he crept round the shore, found her clothes and snatched them away.

After some time, the Heavenly Maidens all climbed out of the water, got dressed and, one by one, rose back into the sky.

But the lady whose clothes he had stolen was left behind, alone. She wrapped her long black hair around herself, sank to the ground, and burst into tears.

At that point, the farmer plucked up courage to come out of hiding and speak to her. They talked all through the long night. She told him she was the Goddess of Weaving, but she hated living in Heaven because of her grandfather, who was unbearably strict. He told her she was the nicest person he had ever met. By the time morning broke, they had indeed fallen madly in love with each other. She was very keen to stay on Earth with him, and to get married.

So they did, and very happy they were too. The goddess carried on with her weaving work, which she was very proud of. People were queuing up to buy her beautiful cloth, so she earned plenty of money for the two of them. They used this to buy some better farm land (not forgetting a smart new shed for the good old ox to sleep in). Now they weren't poor any more. Soon they had two lovely children, a son and a daughter, and their happiness knew no bounds.

But – oh misery! – up in Heaven, the Weaving Goddess's severe old grandfather was stirring up trouble. He stomped around, shouting that a girl had no right to choose a husband for herself. He raged on and on about the disgrace she had brought upon her family by marrying a mere mortal, especially one who was so poor. And how dare she misuse her divine weaving skills to earn *money* – like a mortal peasant woman!

He went on and on about it, until his complaints reached the Jade Emperor himself. At this point, matters were taken out of his hands.

A detachment of Heavenly Guards was rushed down to Earth. Without delay, they seized the goddess out of her own home, took her prisoner, and flew her straight up to Heaven!

The farmer and their two children were there and saw everything. But no ordinary mortal can possibly stop the soldiers of the gods. The family were distraught with grief.

As they tried to comfort each other, the old ox began bellowing urgently from his stall. The farmer ran to him.

"Look," said the ox, "whatever you do, don't despair. Instead, go and fetch the two largest baskets you can find, quick as you can. Pop your children into them, tie them onto the ends of a pole, and hitch the lot up onto your shoulders. Then grab hold of my tail, all shut your eyes – and I'll do the rest."

The farmer rushed off to do as the ox said. No sooner were they all ready with their eyes shut than – wooosh! – they found the ox whisking them up through the sky and heading for Heaven.

Faster and higher they rose. Soon they could see the heavy gates of Heaven looming just ahead. On the other side, the gentle goddess was probably struggling with the guards. Any minute now, they would be able to see her . . .

But they had been spotted! Every soldier in Heaven was already on emergency alert to keep them out; and at that very moment, the Jade Emperor was rising from his throne.

The Jade Emperor stretched out his hand. In a flash, he had created a broad river of stars right across the sky. It was the Milky Way.

The Weaving Goddess was stranded on one side; the farmer and their children on the other. It was as wide as eternity; and there was no way across.

The farmer buried his head in his hands and wept. But his little daughter said, "Father, I have found a ladle in my basket. Why don't we use it to scoop all the water out of this river?"

Although the idea was quite hopeless, the unhappy farmer seized upon it at once. The children jumped down from their baskets to help, scooping out more water with their bare hands.

But the Milky Way went on flowing, fast and deep, fast and deep.

However, when the Jade Emperor saw what they were trying to do in their desperation, even his cold heart melted a little.

He turned the farmer and the goddess each into an especially bright star, one on either side of the Milky Way. The children became two smaller stars next to their father. You can still see them all up there if you look.

Then he issued a special decree, allowing them to visit each other once a year, on the seventh day of the seventh month. That's when all the magpies on Earth fly up into the sky. They make a bridge across the Milky Way, and the little family run across it into each other's arms. Then for a short time they remember how happy they used to be, and the gentle goddess makes rain fall on the Earth she loves, as she weeps many tears of joy.

Darkness

Dajian and Shejian had scarcely been married for six months when the terrible darkness began.

First there was thunder. Then the sky was smothered by black clouds. Finally, the sun disappeared; and it did not come back.

Night fell, and with it came more thunder. The moon seemed to tumble out of the sky. It too vanished as if it were gone for ever.

From that time, both day and night always stayed completely dark. It was like living in a gloomy cave. No-one could see anything. The crops wilted, the flowers shrivelled up, the leaves fell off the trees. Pigs, hens and dogs staggered blindly round the village like troubled ghosts. The people turned pale and sickly; everyone was hungry and afraid.

But Dajian and Shejian were different. Their love was still young and strong: they believed that, together, they could do anything.

"Let's go and find out what has happened to the sun and the moon," said Shejian. Dajian agreed. So they packed two small bags of rice and, hand in hand in the darkness, set off to try and save the world.

They walked on and on, over mountains and across plains, to a place where neither had ever been before. Here they came to a lake where their hearts rose with unexpected hope. For suddenly, they could see each other. And the water itself seemed to be glowing with a strange light.

They ran closer. The light grew steadily brighter. Soon they could see properly for the first time in months, and what they saw made them both catch their breath. The sun and the moon were both bobbing about on the surface of the lake, as if they were two enormous play-balls of gold and silver!

Dajian and Shejian stood and stared in wonder. As they did, the air filled with steam and roaring. Then two great dragons broke the surface of the water. One picked up the sun in its claws; the other grabbed the moon. The next moment, they were tossing them about to each other in a wild, mad game.

Hours seemed to pass. At last the dragons dropped the shimmering balls back into the water, then disappeared into the depths.

"Well, my love," said Dajian, "we have found the sun and moon all right. But how ever will we get them back? *I* am certainly not strong enough to fight two dragons and win."

"Never mind," said Shejian, "let's keep searching. I have always believed that if you have a problem the gods will point you towards the answer, if you know how to read the signs. For example – look."

She pointed towards a huge boulder standing on the slope of the hill. A thin wisp of pale blue smoke was curling out from behind it.

"Maybe that is there to guide us," said Shejian.

"Well, we can soon find out," said Dajian. He put his shoulder to the stone and heaved it to one side. Where it had stood, a long dark tunnel opened into the hill. Far, far along it they could just make out a tiny orange glow, like the embers of a fire.

Clasping each other's hands for comfort, they crept in and walked towards it.

Soon they found themselves in a large, cavernous room with walls of rock. It was furnished with a rough bed, a table and a stool. In one corner was a stove. A very old woman, all wrinkled and bent, stood beside it, poking half-heartedly at the coals. She looked up sharply as they came in, and brandished the red-hot poker at them.

"Oh, don't hurt us!" cried Shejian, "we have come so far . . . Please . . . we were hoping you could help us."

"Help you?" replied the old woman crustily. "How ever could *I* help you?"

So Shejian told her about their quest to return the sun and the moon back to the sky. The old woman seemed to know nothing of the darkness; but when she heard about the dragons, her mouth tightened.

"So that wicked pair are up to their tricks again," she muttered. Then, out loud she said, "I had better warn you, my children, that these are not the usual run of dragons. They have turned their backs on true dragons' work such as making rain and guarding the rivers and seas. No, these are bad ones – so bad that the Dragon Kings of the Four Oceans banished them for ever to this bleak and lonely lake.

"I had better also tell you this: when I was young like you, they were already making trouble. Like you, I was determined to get the better of them. I tried hard; but I failed."

"What did you do?" asked Dajian.

"I poured a whole cauldron of boiling oil into their lake here, that's what I did. I fully intended to kill them; but all I managed to do was burn their skin. My oh my, they were angry then, absolutely seething with anger! They snatched me up and shut me away here in this cave. So that is my story: for fifty years I have been kept a prisoner here, all alone, with only my tears for company."

"Perhaps two of us could succeed in destroying the dragons," said Dajian, "where one was not enough."

The old woman brightened. "Perhaps indeed! Now, listen carefully. When they bring me food, I often overhear the dragons talking, and I have learned that in all the world there are just two things that they are truly afraid of. These are – the magic golden axe and scissors that lie buried not far from here, underneath a great mountain."

"We will go and fetch them," said Shejian at once.

The old woman searched in her memory, and told them the way as best she could. Shejian and Dajian went back down the tunnel and set off. Very soon they came to the mountain. But in the darkness, they did not know where to begin their search.

"Never mind, my love," said Shejian. "Look how far the gods have led us already. Surely now they will help us to find the things we need."

So, side by side, they began to scrabble and dig and delve in the soft earth of the mountainside.

Days and nights passed, though they did not know which was which. Their fingers were blistered and sore, their muscles ached. Still they worked away – until at last a gleam of gold lit up the darkness – and they pulled out the magic axe and scissors!

In their excitement, they forgot how tired they were, and rushed with the tools, back to the old woman's cave. This time she was expecting them, and followed them back down the tunnel and out to the fresh air.

They all sat down to wait on the shore of the lake. By and by, the dragons rose again out of the water. One picked up the fallen sun, the other the fallen moon. With raucous shrieks of laughter, they began to toss them to and fro.

"Throw the axe at them!" hissed the old woman.

Dajian lifted the golden axe high above his head and took aim. It shot into the air. There it turned into a flaming streak of lightning that, for a few seconds, seemed to blaze across the whole sky. Finally it shot down onto the dragons and sliced off their heads.

"Now the scissors!"

This time it was Shejian's turn to throw. As soon as the golden scissors touched the water they came alive and began to slice the dragons' bodies into tiny pieces. The pieces turned into stones and rocks, and the water tossed them up to lie harmlessly all around the shore.

When it was over, Shejian and Dajian clung to each other, trembling. But the old woman said to them, "Your work is not finished yet. You still have to put the sun and the moon back into the sky. Find the dragons' heads and eat their eyes. That will give you the strength to do it."

So Dajian and Shejian searched in the darkness until they found the severed dragons' heads. They swallowed one eye each. At once they both grew tall and strong as giants. In this shape, they stooped awkwardly down towards the lake. Dajian picked up the sun and Shejian picked up the moon. Gently and carefully they hung them up to shine in the branches of the very tallest pine trees.

And at once all the light came back into the world.

The Palace
of Boundless Cold

Once a boy found an injured swallow lying by the side of the road. It lay twittering pitifully, and trying helplessly to move its broken wing. The boy picked it up and carried it home. There he laid it in a box lined with a scrap of old silk, and cared for it gently and kindly for many days.

In the fullness of time, the bird's wing healed. The boy's joy at having nursed it better was tinged with sadness, for he knew now that it must fly away and become wild again.

But the swallow did not forget him. A few days later, it came back to his house and waited on the doorstep until he came out. In its beak, it carried a yellow pumpkin seed. It dropped this at the boy's feet. Then it flew away for good.

The boy planted the seed in his garden. Very quickly, it grew into a strong plant. It flowered, and then began to form a single fruit. This pumpkin seemed to grow fatter and firmer almost as he watched it.

When at last it was ripe, he picked it and cut it open. He was astonished to find a pile of gold and silver coins tumbling out.

It did not take long for news of what had happened to spread right round the village. Everyone was pleased: his family, though hard working, had always been rather poor, and all this money would make things easier for them. Besides, it was good to know that saving even such a tiny, insignificant creature, might earn a lucky reward from Heaven.

But in every village there is always a bad apple. Here, it was another lad, about the same age as the first, who happened to live almost next door to him. To put it bluntly, he was terribly greedy, and burned with envy when he heard about the gold and silver. He decided to waste no time in trying to win something similar for himself.

So he found a small bird of his own, and threw a stone at it – deliberately. The poor thing fell down and broke both its legs: it must have been in terrible pain. The boy picked it up and took it inside. From this point, he made a great public fuss and show of nursing it back to health.

As soon as the bird was recovered, he sent it flying off. Then he settled down to wait for his reward.

Sure enough, a few days later, it returned to him and dropped a pumpkin seed at his feet.

The boy rushed to plant it. Each day as it grew and developed into a fruit, he gloated over it, imagining the fortune that would soon be his. The other villagers tutted and shook their heads over him, but he took no notice.

At last the fruit was ripe. With trembling hands, he picked it and cut it open on the spot.

The two halves split open, as they had done for the first boy; but there was no treasure inside this one. Instead, out stepped a stern old gentleman with a long white beard and the formal robes of a government official.

He stared coldly at the boy.

"So," he exclaimed, "you are the person who has such a longing for gold and silver, eh? Well, if that is what you want so badly, you had better come along this way with me."

He seized the lad by the hand. Just then, the runners of the pumpkin began to grow and turn into a towering ladder that led straight up into the sky. Pulling the boy behind him, the gentleman stepped briskly onto the bottom rung and began to climb steadily up. All the while, the wretched boy struggled to be free, but the stern old gentleman held him in an iron grip.

Only once, he dared to look down. To his horror, he saw that below them, the rungs of the ladder had shrivelled up and fallen off: there was no escape.

On and on they climbed, into darkness. Then at last they stepped off the ladder, and entered an extraordinary place that was dazzlingly bright, yet bitterly cold.

Now they set off along a long straight empty road made of white jade.

"Where . . . where are we, Sir?" whispered the boy, as he tried to catch his breath.

"On the moon of course."

"The moon! Oh! And . . . please, Sir, where are we going to?"

"To the Palace of Boundless Cold."

At last they reached the road's end. Before them, stood a vast building. Its walls were solid gold. Its windows were pure silver.

The old gentleman stopped.

"I trust that this satisfies you? There is more gold and silver here than most people could ever dream of."

The boy looked around. Everything was utterly still and silent. There seemed to be no-one else, and nothing alive. The coldness of the air was rapidly seeping into him, freezing his bones, his blood and his very heart.

"Please, Sir," he said, "I think . . . there has been a mistake. I . . . I . . . Can I go home now?"

"Ohoh!" exclaimed the stern old gentleman. "So you have decided to change your mind, eh?" He gave a dry laugh that sent a shiver down the boy's spine. "Well, hmmm . . . I might consider letting you off after all; but first you must do a little job for me."

He led the boy round a corner of the palace to what seemed at a glance to be a small cinnamon tree. But when he examined it more carefully, the boy saw that its trunk and branches were formed of gold, and its leaves were all glittering precious stones.

The stern old gentleman handed him a silver axe.

"You may use this to try and cut down the tree," he said. "If you succeed, then I will allow you to go home at once; and even to take the tree with you. You can see for yourself, it is laden with enough riches to satisfy your greed for the rest of your life."

"Supposing I don't want to be rich any more, Sir?" asked the boy hoarsely. "Supposing I don't want the tree?"

"You should have thought of that before you deliberately injured that innocent little bird," replied the old gentleman. "It is too late to change your fate now. So take this axe at once, if you please, and begin the task you have been set."

With a heavy sigh, the boy took the axe, swung it back and at once cut a large notch into the golden trunk.

"This is easy after all," he thought to himself. But just then, he felt a dreadful pain in his shoulders.

Swinging round, he found that he was being attacked by an enormous white cockerel.

"Go away!" he yelled, and chased if off with his axe.

He returned to the golden tree, hoping another blow or two might fell it. But to his horror, the notch he had already cut into the trunk had completely disappeared.

Again he struck it with his axe. Again he was attacked by the fierce white cockerel. Again he chased it away, and again he found that the mark he had made with the axe had totally disappeared.

And again, and again, and again . . .

He's still stuck up there today, frozen into the silvery light of the Palace of Boundless Cold. The stern old gentleman is still up there with him, watching in icy silence as the boy sweats away at his impossible task.

So if ever you feel like playing a mean trick to get rich quick – look up at the moon and remember him!

The Realms
of the Dragons

The Golden Key

It had scarcely rained for over a year.

Everything was drying up – wells, rivers, springs – and the thirst was something terrible.

The farms were almost dead. All the animals were weak and shrivelled, and the seeds lay like grit in the parched earth. Nothing would grow: soon there would be nothing left to eat.

It was not surprising that Sea-Girl had stopped singing.

Sea-Girl lived on one of the smaller farms. She could sing more beautifully than the sweetest bird. In normal times, her songs floated across the whole valley, cheering everyone up as they worked.

But now the valley was silent; and Sea-Girl had disappeared.

Nobody knew where she had gone. Nobody guessed that she had crept out in the early morning mists to climb Horse Ear Mountain. Up, up to the thick bamboo groves on the top slopes, where the quiet pandas moved among the green light and shadows. What would she find up there?

She found nothing until she reached the very top of the mountain . . . climbed over the peak, which dipped beyond into a broad plateau . . . and then – she came upon a lake. Water! Wonderful, clear, clean, cool, sweet water – more and much better than she had seen or touched or tasted for over a year!

She knelt – dipped in a finger – then scooped up sparkling handfuls and drank deeply.

When she looked up, a wild goose came gliding over the lake and perched upon a rock some distance away. An eerie shiver ran down her spine: the goose was watching her.

She walked towards it. Soon she saw that its perch was no ordinary rock, but a pair of enormous stone gates.

"Sea-Girl," hissed the goose. "These are the Water Gates. Imagine, if only you could open them – the sparkling water would run through them, out of the lake and straight down into your valley. The rivers and wells would fill up, and the fields would turn green again. No-one would be thirsty or hungry any more."

"But how can I open the gates?" asked Sea-Girl.

"Ah," hissed the goose, "first – first – first . . . you must find the Golden Key."

Then, honking mournfully, it disappeared into the forest.

"Ask me, ask me, ask me!" chanted another voice.

She spun round, and saw a green parrot looking down at her from the branches of a cinnamon tree.

"Sea-Girl," said the parrot, "it is no good looking for the Golden Key until you have found the Dragon King's third and youngest daughter."

"Oh where?" cried Sea-Girl; but the parrot had already flown away.

She turned and walked back into the bamboo forest. Very soon, a peacock alighted before her and began to strut about, displaying his beautiful tail.

"It is not 'where?', Sea-Girl, but 'how'," he said. "And 'how' is easy: you must sing! Go back to the shore and sweeten your throat with more water. Then do not stop singing until the Dragon King's third and youngest daughter comes to you."

So Sea-Girl did as the peacock told her. She sat down and sang until her voice was hoarse. By then the sun was turning red and sinking behind the distant slopes.

The waters of the lake began to stir and ripple. Slowly, the Dragon King's third daughter came rising out. Her body shimmered like a rainbow: one moment a dragon, the next transformed into a young woman, her necklace of water droplets sparkling with golden sunset fire.

"Those are very fine songs," said the Dragon Princess. "I wish you would teach them to me."

"If I teach you my songs," replied Sea-Girl, "would you grant me a wish in return?"

"I could try," laughed the Dragon Princess. "What – or who! – is your heart's desire?"

"Oh, it is nothing romantic," said Sea-Girl. "All I want is to end the drought before all my people die of thirst. And for this, Princess, I need the Golden Key to open up the Water Gates."

"Now that is quite a difficult wish to grant," said the Dragon Princess thoughtfully. "You must realise that the Golden Key is not mine to give you. It belongs to my father, the Dragon King, and so does every drop of water in this lake. He would be fearfully angry if a mere mortal girl like you tried to steal anything that is his.

"Besides, the Golden Key lies in my father's treasure room, and this in turn lies in the deepest heart of our crystal palace. It is guarded by a huge and fierce old eagle, who is under strict orders to kill anyone who tries to steal the treasure."

Sea-Girl's heart sank.

"Neverthless, we will attempt it together," said the Dragon Princess. "But you will have to be both patient and brave."

Then she dived back into the lake.

Sea-Girl waited. By and by, the waters began to froth and bubble as if some terrible volcanic storm were exploding from its depths. Sea-Girl jumped up and hid behind a tree – not a moment too soon, for this time the mighty Dragon King himself came rising out of the water! The wind rushed with his powerful wing-beats as he soared up and away into the sky, taking the direct road to Heaven.

He had scarcely disappeared before the Dragon Princess was back and calling urgently, "Come quickly – here is your chance!"

She took Sea-Girl's hand and pulled her straight down into the cold, clear water. There was no time to gasp for breath, for almost at once they were at the bottom, facing the great, heavy door of the crystal palace. It swung shut behind them, and she found herself breathing air as fresh as a spring morning.

The Dragon Princess led her through light, airy halls, on and on, past towering glass pillars and sparkling fountains. Finally, they stopped by another door, fitted with many strong locks, and even larger and heavier than the first.

The Dragon Princess began to knock and bang on it until her pale knuckles were sore and bruised. All of a sudden, the door opened. The way was blocked by an enormous eagle with angry yellow eyes.

"Ohoh, Princess!" he shrieked, opening and closing his great wings, and stabbing his hooked beak into the air. "Have you got your father's permission to disturb me?"

"There is no need to tell him Sir," replied the Dragon Princess brazenly. "I have only brought my friend to visit you. She is a beautiful singer, and she has come to cheer up your dreary day."

The eagle peered down at Sea-Girl. He was horribly ugly and menacing. Yet she swallowed her fear and began to sing again.

Very soon, the eagle was nodding his head and tapping his huge claws in time with the music. Then his heavy eyelids drooped. Swaying as she sang, he fell at last into a peaceful sleep.

"Now!" cried the Dragon Princess, and Sea-Girl squeezed past the great bird and into the treasure room.

Inside, it was dark apart from a single, flickering lamp. Yet the whole place sparkled with colour, for the flame was reflected from countless tumbling piles of precious metals and stones. Right in the middle was a plain wooden box; and inside the box lay the Golden Key.

Sea-Girl rushed to pick it up. Then she ran back out through the door. The Dragon Princess seized her hand again and together they fled the crystal palace and rose swiftly back up through the lake.

Water streamed off them in the moonlight as they raced to the Water Gates. Sea-Girl threw up her hands in dismay when they got there, because she could see no lock in which to turn the Key. But the Dragon Princess took it from her with a smile and instead used it to tap three times upon the stone gates.

At the third tap, they burst open. At once, water came gushing out, and down, down the mountain.

In the silence of the night they heard it: a new, full river, rushing down to the parched valley below. Sea-Girl closed her eyes, imagining how it would turn the land rich and green again . . .

But when she looked up, the night had darkened and a chill wind had risen. Wings beat loudly then stopped. The Dragon King had returned!

"Who dares to steal my water?"

"Father," said the Dragon Princess softly, "it was me."

The Dragon King breathed out white, angry vapours.

"You? But you are only a young girl! How dare you meddle with my powers, and touch things that only kings may deal with? Go from here! I banish you – you are no longer my daughter! Never dare to show your face in the Realms of the Dragons again!"

So the Dragon Princess went down Horse Ear Mountain with Sea-Girl. She didn't care. She went to live with her like a sister. All day long they worked together on the farm, and Sea-Girl taught her to sing every song that she knew. It was much more fun than the lonely life she used to have in the chilly palace under the lake.

And they had plenty of reason for singing. For they kept the Golden Key, hidden away somewhere secret, until they both died; and then the secret was buried with them. Without the Key, the Dragon King had no choice but to leave the Water Gates open; so the valley under Horse Ear Mountain never again suffered the terrible thirst.

The Man
Who Did Dragons' Work

There's this friend of mine – Li Jing his name is – and one day he was out hunting deer in the forest when he got separated from the rest of the party and realised he was completely lost.

It was turning dark, and he couldn't for the life of him remember the way home. He was tired out and starving, and his horse could hardly keep on its legs. Anyway, he went blundering about among the trees and was just short of panicking when he suddenly came to a big clearing with a river running through it; and on the bank he saw this really amazing house.

It was made entirely of white, shimmering crystal – a huge mansion, very grand. It looked a fine enough place to spend the night.

Li Jing tethered his horse and went up to bang on the door.

It was opened by a servant, who gave him a bit of a funny look and then yelled out, "Mistress, the man has come!" – almost as if he were expected.

The next minute, out came this old lady, very finely dressed, gushing about how pleased she was to see him. It was "Welcome, welcome," a hundred times over. And then she went on: "Before my two sons set off this morning, they told me you were coming. I am afraid that they won't be back for several days; but they were careful to leave full instructions in case Heaven should send orders during your stay. So come inside, my good fellow, have a bite to eat with me; and then you had better take some sleep while you can."

So Li Jing stepped inside, and you can be sure he was bristling all over, wondering what was going on. Well, at first everything was quite straightforward. The old lady led him into the banqueting room and together they sat down to a feast. The only slightly odd thing was that all the food was fish – of every conceivable kind, and cooked in every imaginable delicious way.

Afterwards, servants showed him to his bedroom. There he got his first real inkling of what was coming, when he noticed that all the furniture was decorated by marvellous carvings, each one in the shape of a dragon. But he was so tired that he just climbed into bed and fell fast asleep almost at once.

At midnight he was woken by a loud knocking at the main door of the house. "Open up, in the name of Heaven!"

There were locks rattling and bolts scraping; doors were flung open, voices called urgently, and footsteps hurried up and down. Then there was an uncanny silence for a few minutes, before there came a knock at his own bedroom door.

Li Jing leaped out of bed and opened it. It was the old lady; but in the flickering candle-light her form seemed to be swimming in front of his eyes so that he wasn't quite sure . . . she seemed to be half woman and half . . . dragon!

She handed Li Jing a scroll of paper covered in flowing gold brush strokes and told him to read it.

To the Dragon Lords of the Ling River:
You are hereby commanded to make rain tonight
within a circle of 700 leagues of your palace.
BY ORDER OF THE JADE EMPEROR

"As you know," she said, "my sons are both a thousand miles away tonight. But they told me to expect a nobleman who would arrive in their absence, and that he would be bound to agree to do their work. Mr Li – that man must surely be you!"

"Oh yes, it's me all right," replied Li Jing without hesitation. The old rogue! – He swears he stayed completely poker-faced all the way through. "Madam," he said, really playing along now, "I am honoured."

So the dragon-lady led him outside and clapped her hands. Almost at once a beautiful white horse appeared, seemingly out of nowhere; followed by a servant carrying a small jar made of the finest pale green jade.

Li Jing climbed onto the horse, which was what seemed to be expected of him, and the dragon-lady handed him the jar.

"This horse is the Rainmaker," she told him. "She will carry you above the clouds. Every so often she will stop and neigh, and when she does you must shake one drop from this jar onto her mane. You will see for yourself what happens next."

Li Jing rode off with a great flourish. It wasn't long before the Rainmaker was flying high, high, right up above the dark night. Then she began to stop, here and there, throwing back her head and neighing. Each time, Li Jing shook out a drop from the jade jar onto her wonderful thick, glossy mane. And, as soon as it touched her, the clouds beneath them burst open and it began to rain.

So there you are: that's how the weather happens.

This went on for what seemed like hours, although Li Jing says he was enjoying himself so much, he wouldn't have cared if it had been days. But at last all the magic stuff in the jade jar seemed to be used up, and the Rainmaker did an about-turn in the sky and then galloped back to the crystal mansion – faster even than the wind, Li Jing says.

When they got there, dawn was coming up, and the old dragon-lady was waiting outside for him, all ready to pay him for his services. (I'll tell you more about that in a minute.) So Li Jing took his fee, handed over the Rainmaker to a groom, had a quick bite of breakfast, found his own horse, and set off for home. Now that it was daylight again, the track seemed to open up before him, and he found the way quite easily.

I could see you looking more and more sceptical as I told you all this – so let's go back to that payment. To be frank, I didn't believe a word of Li Jing's extraordinary story either, until he let me see and touch what the old lady had given him. After that, I didn't need any more convincing.

It was a very large purse made of the most exquisite scarlet silk, and embroidered all over with pure gold thread. Inside . . . well, it was crammed full with pearls. But such pearls! They were unbelievably big, and they shone with such a translucent, creamy light. Each single one must have been absolutely priceless. If only you could see them with your own eyes, you'd know . . .

They could only have come from a dragon.

The Hot Pig
and the Dragon Princess

There was a young man nicknamed Baldhead (you can imagine why) who went out and bought himself a young piglet. He pampered it and fed it on lots of tasty scraps, but there was something strange about the creature, for it never seemed to grow any bigger. Worse than that, after a while, its skin shrivelled up and turned a sickly yellow. Baldhead got very depressed about it and wondered whether to put it down, but somehow he never had the heart.

One day, Baldhead and the pig were sitting in the garden together when a foreign traveller came passing by.

"Hello there!" he called. "That's a very fine and unusual pig you've got. Is it for sale? If it is, I'll offer you a hundred silver pieces for it."

Baldhead stared at him open-mouthed. "Did you say a *fine* pig? What on earth do you mean?"

The traveller leaned on the wall and spoke in a confidential whisper. "My friend, don't you realise that this is an extremely rare *ocean-warming* pig? Look . . . I can see you're a poor and honest sort of person, and could make much better use of the thing than me, so I'll let you into its secret.

"Put the pig into a cooking pot, take it down to the seashore and light a fire under it (it won't come to any harm). As the pig water gets hot, so will the sea. When the water boils, the sea will also boil. When the pot has boiled dry, the sea water will also have boiled completely away, and the secret realms that lie on the ocean bed will be exposed. Just think what treasures you might find there!"

And with that, the traveller said goodbye and went on his way.

Baldhead did not waste a single minute. He grabbed the pig, a pot and a bundle of firewood, and rushed down to the shore. Sweating with excitement, he did all that the stranger had said.

Within a short time, the pot was boiling and steaming – and so, indeed, was the sea! Yes, the water level was really starting to fall away . . . and what was that coming at him out of the waves? It looked like . . . it really was . . . a real dragon king!

"Stop this wicked trick at once," roared the Dragon King, "before my royal palace collapses!"

Poor Baldhead was paralysed with fright. "What . . . what . . .?" he stammered. But at last he recovered his senses enough to shout back, "What will you give me if I do stop it?"

"Anything," replied the Dragon King, "anything you choose!"

So Baldhead extinguished the fire under the pot. At once, the water stopped boiling and so did the sea. The magic pig jumped out and ran away, never to be seen again.

Then the Dragon King clapped his hands so that the waves parted to reveal a broad golden road.

"Come this way," he said. "Be my guest for a few days; and then I will let you choose something to take home."

Baldhead followed him down into the dragon kingdom. Its splendour was truly beyond his wildest dreams. Twice a day he sat down to magnificent banquets where he ate and drank as much as he wanted. He slept on soft, scarlet couches. He was waited upon by courteous fish servants who were attentive to his every need.

It was one of these servants who gave him some good advice. "When the king offers you your leaving gift," he said, "forget about gold, silver or jewels. Instead, make sure you ask for the porcelain flower vase which stands there upon the main table."

"Why ever should I want that?" asked Baldhead. But the servant only smiled and winked secretively.

Well, thought Baldhead, each thing that happens to me seems stranger than the last. And he decided to do as the servant suggested.

The Dragon King's face darkened for a moment when Baldhead asked for the vase. But a promise must be kept. So he placed it into Baldhead's hands, urging him always to treat it with care, and sent him on his way.

Baldhead went home. The next morning, he set off to work as usual. He came back late, tired and hungry – but what a surprise awaited him: someone had been into his house and cooked a delicious meal! The table was set, and it was all ready to eat. Yet whoever it was had disappeared.

The next day, it was just the same. Baldhead was as puzzled as he was pleased. "I must get to the bottom of this," he said to himself.

So on the third day, instead of going to work, he hid inside a cupboard, watching to see what happened.

By and by, the flower vase began to shiver and quiver, to shimmer and shake and dazzle, until he could scarcely bear to look at its brightness. He blinked and rubbed his eyes.

When he opened them again, the vase was no longer there: it had turned into a mysterious young woman!

Baldhead leaped out at her. "Who are you?" he demanded. "What's going on?"

The young woman smiled back at him calmly. "I am the Dragon Princess," she replied. "Several years ago, a wicked magician who had a quarrel with my father turned me into a vase. Because you admired me enough to care for me, even in that lifeless form, the spell has been partly broken to allow me to escape from it for a few hours each day. I am so grateful, that the least I can do is to cook your evening meal for you."

"Well," said Baldhead wonderingly, "well, well, well! And what must I do to free you from the spell entirely?"

"You would have to marry me," said the Dragon Princess.

Baldhead could hardly believe his luck. Here he was, at least as poor as the next fellow, and not exactly the most handsome of men either; and an enchanting dragon princess was almost begging him to become her husband!

He fixed up the wedding as fast as he could. Afterwards, she never turned into the vase again. Baldhead was absolutely besotted with love for her. Only one thing spoiled his happiness: he couldn't help feeling that his humble shack was a poor home for a woman who was both immortal and of royal blood.

When he plucked up courage to tell her what troubled him, the Dragon Princess just laughed. "Oh, that's no problem at all. Why ever didn't you mention it before?"

She went straight out into the yard, took a silver hairpin out of her long, thick hair and used it to trace a series of lines across the grass.

At once there was a crash of thunder and the shack crumbled into a pile of dust. Next, a whirlwind blew up and carried it away. Finally, the ground cracked open, and out of it sprang an enormous mansion, decorated with the latest style of elaborate ornaments, and surrounded by beautiful gardens.

The Dragon Princess led Baldhead gently inside. He was quite overcome by the splendour of it all.

"Remember, my dear," said the Dragon Princess kindly, "if there's anything else you want, all you have to do is ask."

Now, next door to them lived a man called Zhang. He was rather a nasty piece of work: as greedy as he was wealthy, and he hated anyone to have anything better than himself.

When he saw the magnificent house spring up in place of Baldhead's old hovel, he guessed that magic had been at work. He sent his servant to spy and ask questions. Very soon the fellow came back goggle-eyed, telling Zhang all sorts of rumours about the wondrous Dragon Princess.

The next day, Zhang got into his sedan chair and went round to see Baldhead.

"Watch yourself," he said menacingly, "and most of all, watch that lovely wife of yours. I'm warning you: you'd better make a moat around this magnificent house of yours in the next three days. Otherwise, I'm going to steal the lady from you!"

When he was gone, Baldhead wailed with despair. But the Dragon Princess said, "Be quiet, my dear, and do as I tell you. Take this gold, and buy a hundred stakes, a hundred robes and a hundred hats. Place the stakes evenly around the house and hang the clothes on top of them. That will put old Zhang in his place!"

Baldhead did everything she said; and sure enough, within three days, their mansion was surrounded by a moat, two metres wide!

Zhang was furious when he saw it. "Don't think your lovely wife is safe from me yet!" he shouted. "I'll give you three more days to fill up the moat with water, otherwise I'm coming to get her."

"Tut tut," said the Dragon Princess, "does he really think we are afraid of him?"

She slipped a pearl off her necklace, popped it into her mouth, and at once was transformed into her dragon shape. She jumped into the moat and began to yawn, making a great spray of water gush out of her mouth.

When this water had filled the moat, she turned back into a woman.

Zhang was more annoyed than ever. "I'm *still* going to get that wife of yours," he yelled, "unless you can grow a thick forest between this moat and your house – in the next three days!"

"That really is impossible," sighed Baldhead. "No-one can grow even a single tree in less than twenty years, let alone a whole forest."

But the Dragon Princess laughed. "Just go and dig up some saplings from the mountain, my dear one, and plant them all round the inner edge of the moat; then leave the rest to me."

Baldhead did it. By the time Zhang next came along, the trees were growing so thickly that they could scarcely hear his latest threats: "I'm still going to get her, I'm still going to snatch her from you, oh yes, oh yes!"

"I know how to shut him up once and for all," said the Dragon Princess. "Go down to the seashore that I came from and call three times with these magic words. My father will send what you need on the waves. Bring it home; but whatever you do, *don't open it*."

By now Baldhead knew that his wife's advice was always to be trusted. He followed her instructions and, as soon as he finished, a huge brass pot rose out of the water and came floating towards him on the tide.

He got back to his mansion, just in time to see a boat rowing across the moat. Zhang got out and hacked a way through the trees to the front door.

"I've come to take your wife now!" he announced when he reached it.

"Give him the pot," hissed the Dragon Princess, who was hiding behind the door.

Baldhead was still terrified, despite the magic. "You're not . . . not . . . having her," he stammered. "But you can have . . . have this instead." And he thrust the pot into Zhang's hands.

"Whatever do I want with this silly thing?" said Zhang contemptuously.

"Open it up and you'll see," called the Dragon Princess from her hiding place.

"Was that you, my little beauty?" simpered Zhang, his eyes lighting up at her voice. "I'll certainly open the pot if *you* want me to."

So he lifted off the lid.

First, a weird voice cried out: *"Silly thing, silly thing, do you call all this silly?"*

65

Next a sizzling flame leaped up, straight into Zhang's face. His hair, eyebrows and eyelashes were all so badly singed that they fell out. What a sight he looked then!

Finally, the voice cried again: *"You're the one that's silly, always trying to steal another man's wife!"*

Zhang didn't wait for anything else. He dropped the pot and ran off and away through the forest and across the moat as fast as he could. Perhaps he left the neighbourhood after that: at any rate, he never bothered Baldhead and the Dragon Princess again.

And that's about the end of their story; for no doubt the two of them spent the rest of their days together in happiness and peace.

Roads to Heaven

The Girl
Who Went Her Own Way

Long ago, in the days when nice girls were always supposed to do exactly what their fathers told them, there was a young princess called Miaoshan who decided to go her own way.

For Miaoshan had looked out through the windows of the royal palace, far, far and beyond. She had seen how vast the world was, and how full of many things.

But more than that, she had also gazed through the shifting lights of her mind's eye, deep, deep into her own soul. There she found marvellous powers, and an overwhelming love for all living things, buried within herself like hidden treasure.

She grew strong on the knowledge of what life was, and what she could do.

She learned to say "No" when her mother wanted her to waste time with foolish gossip or idle palace games. She took off her priceless jewels and threw them outside to the poor ragged peasants who laboured without cease in the fields around the palace. And when her father, the King, told her she had better change her ways and grow up, because he was busy finding a rich prince to become her husband, she stood up straight and said "No" to that too.

"I'm not getting married," said Princess Miaoshan firmly. "Not ever. I want a different kind of life. I've decided to join the Buddhists. I'm going to become a nun."

Her father turned pale with rage and horror.

"Join the Buddhists!" he roared. "Do you realise what a weak, pathetic bunch of people they are? Oh, by Heaven: here I am with the biggest, fiercest army in the whole world – and my own daughter plans to run off with a load of namby-pambies who want to abolish war!"

"Listen dear," said the Queen. "Think of the delicious food we've brought you up on: fine roast duck, juicy suckling pork . . . Don't you realise that the Buddhists won't let you have a single taste of meat, not ever again. You must be crazy! If you join a nunnery, they'll take away all your comforts, and make you spend the rest of your life sitting under some lonely tree, staring at your navel and meditating. Think of all the fun and parties you could be enjoying instead, when we've married you off to a nice, wealthy prince."

But Princess Miaoshan only shrugged and said, "Personally, I think that war is cruel and pointless. Eating meat makes me feel ill because it comes from animals, and they are my sisters and brothers. And I absolutely hate wasting my time on what you call 'fun'. All the things that the Buddha taught are the very same things that I believe in. Listen father: you think you can force me to do what you want, but you are wrong."

At these words, the King lost all control of his temper. He shouted for maid-servants and guards to come at once. He ordered them to strip Princess Miaoshan of all her warm clothes; to take her outside to the palace courtyard; and to lock the doors and gates tightly upon her. There he forced her to stay for many days and nights, wearing only her thin underclothes, and with no food or drink.

Every afternoon a messenger was sent out to ask if she would now give up her mad ideas and fix a date for her wedding. And each time he returned with the same answer: "No."

At last, the Queen herself went out to see her. She found Miaoshan sipping dew from a lotus leaf and sharing a handful of seeds with a small mouse. With a happy smile, she invited the Queen to sit beside her on a soft hummock of grass.

"Well, my daughter," said the Queen shortly, "whatever are we to do with you?"

"Just let me go to the Nunnery of the White Bird, please," replied Princess Miaoshan. "Then I'll be out of sight, and you and father can forget all about me."

With a sigh, the Queen left her, and went off to discuss things with the King. After much arguing and many tears, they agreed at last that the awkward girl should be banished in accordance with her own wishes.

So, the next morning, Miaoshan was allowed to go away. She left behind everything that she owned: all her clothes, ornaments and jewels.

Then she walked alone through the forest to the nunnery. There she took up the harsh, humble life of a Buddhist holy woman.

Now she had her own way; now she was really happy.

But the cruel King was not. He wanted to punish her because she was different, because she challenged the settled order of things, because her ideas disturbed him. He wanted her to suffer.

He sent spies to the nunnery to find out if a diet of plain boiled rice, and a routine of scrubbing floors and meditation had wiped the smile off her face.

They came back with the news that everyone in the nunnery spoke well of her kindness and cheerful ways. When he heard this, the King's heart was flooded with evil thoughts.

He sent the spies back, carrying burning torches. On his orders, they threw them into the nunnery. The building caught fire at once. It seemed that within minutes the whole place would be blazing to the ground, with Miaoshan and the other women all burned alive inside it.

But up in Heaven, the Buddha himself was watching. He took a handful of water and threw it down to Earth as a heavy shower of rain. At once, the fire was quenched, so that Miaoshan and her sister nuns were saved.

When the King heard of this, his fury knew no bounds. He sent soldiers out to seize his daughter; and then without further ado, they cut her throat and killed her.

Like all beings, Miaoshan was dead in the body only: her soul still lived. It went down into the dim regions of the Underworld, where King Yama weighed up rewards and punishments for all the souls of the dead.

He had never seen a soul like Miaoshan's before!

For it shone with a dazzling, sweet light that chased away all the darkness of Hell. Even the stern, immovable faces of the assistant Judges of Death were brightened by it.

It sent the whole place into turmoil. Hell was supposed to be grim and terrible, not cheerful. King Yama feared that his authority was under threat. He sent an urgent message up to the Buddha in Heaven, asking him to remove this disconcerting soul at once.

The Buddha chuckled to himself when he got the message. He sent down a magic tiger to carry Miaoshan's poor, wounded body to the island of Putuo, and then to lick it until it was healed. A lotus flower floated behind, carrying her soul to the same place. There her body and soul were joined together again, and Miaoshan was made whole.

In the peace of that island she found *Nirvana*: perfect knowledge and perfect wisdom. She learned to understand all things in the Universe; she became at one with all rhythms, and she settled her way in harmony with the great flow.

Then Miaoshan rose to Heaven. The Buddha was waiting to welcome her, and hurried her along to the palace of the Jade Emperor. There a grand ceremony was held. The Jade Emperor took away her old name and announced: "I make you new: and I name you Guanyin, my Goddess of Mercy. May your fame spread as widely as your kindness! From now on, you may go in freedom which ever way you want to, and take on any shape which serves you best."

Ah, Guanyin, how everyone longs for your footsteps to pass close by! For you understand all sadness, pain and suffering; and how warm is the comfort that you bring!

Cakes and Kitchens

"Hush! Hold your tongue and don't you ever dare to say such things in the kitchen again! Whatever will Zao Zhun think?"

"Zao Zhun?"

"The Kitchen God. That's his picture, pinned up above the stove. He watches over us all the time, you know, and listens to every word we say. Look, I know you're from outside the Middle Kingdom, and don't understand our ways, but I must beg you to respect Zao Zhun. You see, he reports on us to the Jade Emperor himself, every New Year; and if he hears such disgusting things said in front of him, we'll get into terrible trouble for it."

"So what will happen?"

"Oh, I don't know – some kind of bad luck that's for sure. Here, take this honey and smear it over his lips. That's right. It'll sweeten his words about us when he next goes up to Heaven. He loves anything sweet. It's on account of the cakes, when he was just an ordinary man down here on Earth, long, long ago. Look, make yourself comfortable and I'll tell you his story . . ."

Zao Zhun was a stone-mason who always worked hard, always told the truth, and always treated other people kindly. You might think that Heaven would have rewarded him with an easy life, but not a bit of it! Instead, no matter how hard the wretched man worked, he just seemed to get poorer and poorer.

Zao Zhun had a wife, whom he loved very dearly, and she loved him. But he just couldn't afford to keep them both. There was no honest way that the woman could earn her own living either, and they began to fear that one or both of them would starve to death.

In the end, they decided the only thing to do was to break up their marriage. In great sorrow, they kissed each other and said goodbye. The good woman went off and married another man who was rather rich, whilst Zao Zhun settled down to live a bleak life all on his own.

The years passed. Zao Zhun travelled about, here and there, looking for work. One day he was called to do a few repairs in the house of a rich merchant. He had no idea that this man was in fact the new husband of his beloved ex-wife!

No, even though he saw his wife at the house, he did not recognise her, for her looks were totally transformed by her new life of luxury and wealth. But in her heart she had not changed at all. As soon as she saw Zao Zhun again, she knew that he would always be her only true love, and she was overwhelmed with tenderness for him.

However, she was very afraid of her new husband, who was as short-tempered as he was rich. She wracked her brains for a way of helping Zao Zhun without rousing her new husband to violent anger.

At last she had an idea. She baked some tasty sesame cakes and hid a gold coin inside each one. When Zao Zhun had finished his work, she gave them to him as if they were just an ordinary, polite gift for his journey.

Just at that moment, her new husband came storming into the room with a sour expression on his face. The good woman had no chance to whisper the cakes' secret to Zao Zhun, nor to reveal who she really was.

So the stone-mason went off, carrying the little bundle of cakes, but totally ignorant of the treasure that they contained. Soon he came to a tea-house and went inside for a drink. As he sipped it, he put the cakes on the table beside him. He thought he would keep them for supper, for all his storage pots at home were quite empty.

There was another man sitting at the next table, and he was poor too. When he saw Zao Zhun's cakes, his stomach began to rumble.

"Excuse me, my friend," said he, "but would you by any chance be able to spare a small bite to eat?"

"Help yourself," said Zao Zhun generously.

Well, the other man bit into a cake, and at once his teeth hit something hard. He waited until Zao Zhun turned the other way, and then he took it out of his mouth to examine it. Ohoh, gold! He was a crafty, quick-witted fellow, and he soon guessed that there might be a coin hidden in every cake. He also guessed that Zao Zhun had no idea about them.

So he sidled over and offered to buy the lot for a small sum. Zao Zhun, ignorant and trusting as he was, agreed.

And that was it: the cakes and gold coins were all lost in a few minutes – and with them, his only chance of escaping from poverty. Some time later, his ex-wife managed to smuggle out a letter to him, asking how he had used the gold. You can imagine what a bitter taste it left in his mouth when he realised what he had lost!

However, when he died, the Jade Emperor gave him the reward he deserved. He appointed Zao Zhun to be Kitchen God so that he never felt the pangs of hunger again. And he took away the bitterness by making sure that everyone regularly offered him lots of delicious honey and sweets. And there's no danger of him ever being left out of secrets again, for now he lives at the heart of every home, and knows everything that goes on!

Storm Girl

It must be strange to be born with supernatural powers. They seem to unfold themselves as a child learns to walk and talk. To be able to foresee things in the future, to talk with ghosts and ancestors, to travel 'out of the body' . . . it is important to guard such talents carefully, and learn to use them only to do good.

Girls and women tend to have them more than boys and men. For the female essence is *yin*; and *yin* is also all things mystical. The secret is not to be afraid of them, but to go gently with their flow. Then it is possible even to achieve miracles.

Little Tian Hou was only seven, but already she had such a gift. She lived near the sea, and was alive to its rhythms. When the tide ebbed and flowed, her spirit went with it. She could fly out of her body, and over the waves. In such a state, the sea could never harm her, no matter how rough it was; nor could the wind, nor even thunder or lightning.

She told no-one about it.

Tian Hou's father was a sailor. So were her two grown-up brothers. They all lived with their ageing mother in a little house by the shore.

One day, when the three men were out at sea, a terrible storm blew up. The wind raced and roared and whirled about, whipping up the inky waves into a fury. Torrential rain mixed with the spray. Lightning zig-zagged across the dark sky; thunder rumbled and crashed.

The old woman and the little girl shut themselves inside their house and fastened the door securely against the wildness. They stoked up the fire and sat silently side by side, listening to the storm rattling the walls.

All at once, Tian Hou's eyes glazed. Then she keeled over and fell to the floor as if in a faint. Under her mother's touch, her body felt icy cold and stiff. Yet she was breathing, oh so softly; and softly, softly, her pulse was beating too.

"Tian Hou my child! Oh my sweet little girl!" Over and over, the mother called her. "What is wrong? Where have you gone to? Oh my little Tian Hou, come back, come back!"

Many hours must have passed while the girl lay still and silent, and the woman wailed and called.

At long last, Tian Hou opened her eyes and smiled sadly.

"My brothers are safe," she said. "But I had no time to save Father. You called me and called me so urgently that I had no choice but to come back to you before I could reach him."

"Whatever do you mean?" asked the mother, torn between joy at her daughter's recovery, and foreboding at her words.

"Wait and you will see," said the little girl solemnly.

Some days later, Tian Hou's brothers came home. Their clothes were in tatters and they looked pale and weary. Their mother ran to greet them; but their first words were, "Father is dead."

Then they sat down and told their story.

"That storm," said the older brother, "it was the worst we've ever known. Our ship was tossed about on the waves as if it were no more than a stick of driftwood. We were all clutching each other: even the toughest fellows were sick and screaming. And with each wave someone else was pitched overboard to drown."

"It was even worse than that," said the younger brother. "No-one could describe the horror. But anyway, when there were just us two and Father left alive, this amazing goddess-like apparition suddenly appeared. She was flying above us like . . . like a bird riding on the back of the wind! Before I knew what was happening, she snatched me up in her arms and flew off with me. The next I can remember, I was safe on dry land."

"Then she came back for me," said the first brother. "When I was safe too, she promised to fly back to the sinking ship one more time to rescue Father. We watched her go; but then the darkness of the storm swallowed her up; and she never came back."

Tian Hou listened to their words. Then she said, "It was I who rescued you. I left my body and flew through the storm to you. I tried desperately to save our father too; but Mother kept calling me, over and over, until in the end her call was stronger than my powers." Tears ran down her cheeks. "I am sorry. Maybe if I had explained my powers to you all before, Mother would have left me to my work, and Father could have come home with you too."

News of what Tian Hou could do spread far and wide. People began to talk of her as the 'Little Princess of Magic Powers'.

She was still a young girl when she died. Then her mother and brothers were as proud as they were sad. For they knew that she had gone straight to Heaven and become a real goddess.

Now people prayed to her, and she did what she could to help them. She saved many other sailors from storms and shipwrecks. She held back pirates. She moved amongst the dragon kings; and if ever there was a drought, it was she who persuaded them to end it.

Today they call her the Empress of Heaven, and her compassion spreads as wide as the sea.

The Boys
Who Lost Their Time

Liu Chen and Yuan Zhao were friends as well as cousins; and everything they did, they did together.

One day, their fathers sent them into the hills to fetch some water from a spring. When their buckets were full, the boys left them by the path and went racing off over the grass.

Liu Chen was a fast runner; Yuan Zhao was even faster. It didn't take them long to reach the highest slopes where rare and wonderful wild flowers grew thickly in the shadows of the pine trees. A fine mist came down, and began to close in on them.

"We ought to get back now," said Yuan Zhao nervously.

But Liu Chen tapped him on the shoulder and whispered, "Turn round quietly . . . and look!"

Just behind them, a dark cave opened into the hillside. On either side of the entrance was a large, flat stone. And on each stone was sitting a fairy-man!

Between the fairies a chessboard rested on another stone. The pair were bent over it in deep, silent concentration.

In front of the chessboard was a white hare, jumping up and down, up and down, very fast. And this was the oddest thing of all: as the hare jumped up, all the flowers around the cave opened up their petals; but as it came to rest, the flowers all faded and withered away. It happened so quickly that the boys were dazzled to watch it.

After a while, the right-hand fairy shouted, "Checkmate!" and stood up triumphantly. The other reached across and shook his hand. Then they both noticed the two boys:

"Good Heavens!"

"A couple of young mortals!"

"And how long have you two been spying on us, eh?"

Liu Chen and Yuan Zhao clutched each other in great fright.

"Oh . . . um . . . only for a . . . a few minutes," stammered Liu Chen.

"No, no, it must have been for a few hours," Yuan Zhao corrected him.

At this, the two fairies fell about laughing:

"A few hours!"

"A few minutes – that's even better!"

"If only they knew!"

"If only they realised!"

By and by, the fairies recovered themselves enough to tell the boys:

"Things are not at all what you think they are, oh dear no!"

"You'd better stay here with us now . . ."

". . . For if you go home, no-one will know who you are."

"You're lying!" shouted Yuan Zhao. "Come on, cousin." And the boys turned and ran together down the hillside, through the mist and out of it, as fast as they could.

They came back to the place where they had left their buckets of water. There was no sign of them.

Their hearts were beating very fast now – not just from running, but also with rising fear. They ran on, heading for home.

They came to the place where their village should have been. Indeed, there was a village there – but it was not theirs. For all the houses were totally wrong, totally different . . .

And all the people that they saw were strangers.

They walked up and down the lanes, looking for a face or a place that they recognised; but there were none.

At last they stopped outside a house where two very old men with long white beards were sitting sunning themselves in the yard.

"Hey, urchins," called one of the men, "what are you snooping round here for?"

"Please sir," said Liu Chen, "we're looking for the houses of Liu Chen and Yuan Zhao."

"Well, well, well," said the other old man, "you've come to the very spot all right. This is where the two of them once lived, though their original houses were pulled down about a hundred years ago, and these fine new ones were built in their place."

"A hundred years ago?" cried Yuan Zhao in dismay. "But that's impossible!"

"Impossible?" retorted the first old man. "Don't you argue with your elders, boy! I ought to know the history of this place, seeing as Liu Chen was my ancestor – seven generations ago."

The boys stared at him.

"That's right," said the second old man, "and Yuan Zhao was mine: my great-great-great-great-great-grandfather."

"But *I* am Liu Chen, and look I'm still alive, and only a boy. And *he* is Yuan Zhao!"

At this, the two old men jumped up and waved their walking sticks at them threateningly: "Be off with you, urchins! How dare you insult our ancestors like that! Get away before we beat you black and blue!"

So the boys turned and ran – straight up the hillside again, for they had nowhere else to go. They didn't stop until they got to the place where the fairy-cave was.

There they flopped down on the grass, side by side.

"Listen cousin," said Liu Chen, "I think I understand what has happened. You remember that hare that was jumping up and down in front of the fairies? And how the flowers kept blooming and dying with every leap?"

"I know what you're going to say," replied Yuan Zhao. "That magic hare must somehow have been playing about with Time. It was making the seasons – and the years – rush past as it danced."

"And it jumped up and down hundreds of times," said Liu Chen slowly. "So *hundreds* of seasons must have come and gone!"

"Exactly," agreed Yuan Zhao. "So we should be long dead and buried. Those two bad-tempered old men really were our descendants." He sighed. "And there's no chance that anyone alive *now* will either know us, or want us."

"Those wicked fairies," cried Liu Chen, "it's all their fault!"

"I bet they did it on purpose!" agreed Yuan Zhao. "Just wait till we get them!"

And the two boys began to bang and pound on the hillside by the cave, yelling and screaming at the fairies to come and rescue them. But nothing happened and there was no reply.

That was how the Jade Emperor spotted them, when he peered down to Earth to see what was going on. He called his officials to prepare a report on the two boys, and when he heard their strange, sad story, he took pity on them, and had them whisked up to Heaven at once.

After all they had been through, it seemed only fair to offer them jobs as gods. The boys were thrilled. The Jade Emperor consulted his lists, and found there were two vacancies in the Ministry of Luck. They had to sit exams first, of course; but they had learned so much from their weird experiences, that both passed with flying colours.

Liu Chen became the God of Good Luck, and Yuan Zhao became the God of Bad Luck.

The chances are that you will meet them both, as you walk down Life's long road.

About the People
Who Told these Stories

China and its people

The stories in this book were first told by people from one of the oldest and greatest civilisations in the world. China is a vast country, stretching from Central Asia to the Pacific Ocean. Today it contains one-fifth of the entire world population: over 1,000 million people.

Chinese history can be traced back continuously over 4,000 years. From about 1800 BC until the early 20th century, the country was ruled by a series of dynasties (royal families), headed by successive emperors. They were so successful and powerful that through most of history the Chinese thought of themselves as living in the very centre of civilisation, whilst foreigners were dismissed as ignorant and uneducated barbarians.

The Chinese were the first people in the world to discover and invent many important things – for example, silk, paper, printing, the magnetic compass and gunpowder. They were also the first country to establish a properly qualified 'civil service' of government officials. The Great Wall of China – stretching for 2,400 kilometers and built around 220 BC – is the longest ever man-made structure on Earth.

Although there have been cities in China for thousands of years, most of the people have always been farmers. Many have found it hard to scrape a decent living from the land, particularly as droughts, floods and typhoons are common natural disasters. Even today, three-quarters of the people still live and work in the countryside.

Old Chinese beliefs

The traditional Chinese outlook on life is like a wonderfully rich tapestry into which many different strands and threads have been woven.

Three wise men

Amongst the most important strands are the teachings of three very different wise men from ancient times.

Kong Fuzi ('Venerable Master Kong' – known in Western countries as **Confucius**) lived in the 6th to 5th century BC. He produced a set of moral rules designed to help people live well and happily together. He taught that everyone should be courteous and considerate towards others. In all relationships, the 'superior' person (generally an older male) had a duty to be kind and honest, whilst the 'inferior' one (generally younger and/or female) had to be totally loyal and obedient. Loyalty to one's family was particularly important. In addition, he encouraged people to worship various gods and also the family ancestors.

After his death, the emperors made 'Confucianism' the official religion of China, and it remained so almost until present times. Respectable Chinese people always used Kong Fuzi's teachings as their basic moral code.

Laozi ('The Old Sir') lived around the same time as Kong Fuzi. He wrote a very beautiful and mysterious book called *Daodejing* ('The Way and its Power'), which tries to describe and explain the flowing patterns and rhythms of life and the universe. These patterns and rhythms include two opposite forces, *yin* and *yang*, which are believed to be present in all things. *Yin* includes things female, dark and mysterious, the earth and the moon. *Yang* includes things male, light and active, the sun and the heavens. Mixed together, they produce harmony. Laozi urged his followers to try to live in similar harmony with nature, and not to fight against the flow.

Laozi started the Daoist religion. Long after his death, he became revered as a god and extraordinary legends were told about him. Later, many other ideas were added to his basic teachings. These included the belief that it was possible for ordinary people to obtain immortality, or everlasting life.

The Buddha was not Chinese, but Indian. His real name was Siddhartha Gautama and he lived in the 7th century BC. He is said to have discovered *Nirvana*: that is, perfect peace and perfect understanding of the meaning of life. He achieved this through 'meditation', which involves sitting very quietly and concentrating on one's inner being. He started the Buddhist religion, which is now practised in many countries of the Far East. It teaches that everyone can find *Nirvana* for themselves by their own efforts. It also urges its followers to live good, gentle lives; to stop wasting their energy on selfish desires; and to treat all living creatures with kindness and respect.

By about the 4th century AD Buddhism had become an important part of Chinese religion, and the Chinese came to regard the Buddha as a god.

Gods, goddesses and dragons

The Chinese believed in a great number of **gods and goddesses**. Most of these were once ordinary people who had become divine after death because of something special they had done during their lives. Some of their stories are told in the last section of this book.

The gods and goddesses all lived in Heaven. This was quite different from the wonderful paradise that Westerners have imagined Heaven to be. Instead, it was like a huge government office. And each god and goddess was really rather like a government minister, with a special job to do, particular worldly affairs to look after, and staff to assist him or her.

The most important god, to whom all the others 'reported', was the Jade Emperor. He was like a direct reflection of the Chinese Emperor on Earth: his palace, his court, his army – even his clothes – were almost exact replicas of the Earthly ones. His wife was Queen Mother Wang, who was famous for her special birthday banquets at which she served magic peaches which renewed the gift of everlasting life for all the immortals who ate them.

There were so many gods and goddesses that it would be impossible to mention them all, but here are a few examples: the God of Wealth and Good Fortune; the Three Gods of Happiness; the God of Examinations; the gods of particular places; and the Door Gods who watched over every home.

A particularly well loved goddess was the kind and merciful Guanyin, who was believed to bring babies and heal the sick. And almost every home would contain a picture of Zao Zhun, the Kitchen God, who sent reports to the Jade Emperor about the household's behaviour.

Dragons were also immortal, and mixed with the gods in Heaven. Unlike Western dragons, they were generally well meaning, although they had dangerous tempers. They were particularly connected with water and were believed to bring the rain. Each of the four seas said to surround the Earth had its own Dragon King, as did many lakes and rivers.

Pictures and statues of the main gods and goddesses were kept in special temples, and many people also kept images of their favourites in their own homes. Followers worshipped them with special offerings of food and money, and by burning incense. In return, they expected the gods and goddesses to answer their prayers and help them.

Family, ancestors and spirits

The most important thing in almost everyone's life was their own family. A typical family would be very closely knit, and all members were expected to be completely loyal and dutiful to each other. Respecting and caring for one's parents was considered a particularly important duty. The family head was always the grandfather, who ideally would live with his wife, their sons and their wives, and their grandchildren. As the oldest male, he would be treated with the utmost respect, and everyone would obey him. Elderly people and men were generally regarded as being superior to young people and women.

When a person died, it was believed that his or her spirit continued to live, and that it must be looked after by its living relatives, particularly by any sons. They had to carry out special ceremonies to keep it safe. If they failed to do this, the spirit would become a dangerous and trouble-making 'hungry ghost'.

Most families had a shrine at home dedicated to the spirits of their family ancestors, sometimes going back through numerous generations. They made regular offerings to these spirits, and also made pilgrimages to the family graves.

The supernatural

Sometimes people asked their ancestors for advice before deciding to do something important. In order to 'speak' with them, they consulted professional mediums, who were supposed to be able to carry messages between the living and the spirits of the dead. Women tended to have more talent than men for communicating with ancestors, spirits and deities. This was because women were *yin*, and *yin* was also associated with the supernatural.

The supernatural was very much a part of daily life. People had a strong sense of being in tune with nature, which was felt to be constantly flowing, changing shape and transforming itself as time passed. Spirits, ghosts and magic were considered an inherent part of this.

Dreams were believed to be of particular significance. Sometimes they predicted the future; sometimes they were supposed to show the dreamer something that had actually happened on a different level of consciousness. Fortune telling and foreseeing the future were normal, everyday events.

Links with the past

In 1911 the last Chinese Emperor was overthrown by a revolution. Since 1949 the People's Republic of China – most of the Chinese mainland – has been ruled by the Communist Party, which has forced through a total transformation of society, and banned traditional religion and beliefs.

However, the old traditions are still very much alive in outlying parts of China which have remained outside Communist rule. These include Taiwan (an independent island nation); Hong Kong (a colony of Britain until 1997, now a Special Administrative Region of the People's Republic of China); and Macao (currently a colony of Portugal). The old traditions are also kept up within the large Chinese communities of Thailand, Malaysia, Indonesia, Singapore, Vietnam and many other countries world-wide.

Many of the old myths and folktales in this book are still regularly told. To share them is to enter a rich world of the imagination, where ordinary people frequently may cross paths with gods, goddesses, dragons and strange supernatural forces.

Sources

Cyril Birch, *Chinese Myths and Fantasies* (Oxford University Press, London 1961)

Frena Bloomfield, *The Book of Chinese Beliefs* (Arrow Books, London 1983)

Anthony Christie, *Chinese Mythology* (Paul Hamlyn, London 1968)

Anthony Christie, 'China' in, Richard Cavendish, *Mythology – An Illustrated Encyclopaedia* (Orbis, London 1980)

Wolfram Eberhard, *Folktales of China* (Routledge & Kegan Paul, London 1965)

Brian Hook (ed.), *Cambridge Encyclopaedia of China* (Cambridge University Press 1982)

Joanne O'Brien & Man Ho Kwok, *Chinese Myths and Legends* (Arrow Books, London 1990)

Ou-I-Tai, 'Chinese Mythology' in: *New Larousse Encyclopaedia of Mythology* (Hamlyn, London 1968)

Tao Tao Lui Sanders, *Dragons, Gods and Spirits from Chinese Mythology* (Schocken Books, New York 1983)

E. T. C. Werner, *Myths and Legends of China* (Harrap, London 1922)

E. T. C. Werner, *A Dictionary of Chinese Mythology* (The Julian Press, New York 1961)

Clio Whitaker (ed.), *An Introduction to Oriental Mythology* (Apple Press, London 1989)

Wu Ch'eng-en, *Monkey*, translated from the Chinese by Arthur Waley (George Allen & Unwin, London 1942)